PLATO

SOPHIST

THE PROFESSOR OF WISDOM

The Focus Philosophical Library

PLATO

SOPHIST

THE PROFESSOR OF WISDOM

With Translation,
Introduction, and
Glossary

Eva Brann
Peter Kalkavage
Eric Salem

focus an imprint of
Hackett Publishing Company, Inc.
Indianapolis/Cambridge

Plato
Sophist
©1996 by Eva Brann, Peter Kalkavage, Eric Salem

Focus an imprint of
Hackett Publishing Company

For further information, please address
Hackett Publishing Company, Inc.
P.O. Box 44937
Indianapolis, Indiana 46244-0937

www.hackettpublishing.com

ISBN: 978-0-941051-51-4

20 19 18 17   9 10 11 12 13

The paper used in this publication meets the minimum requirements of
American National Standard for Information Sciences—Permanence of
Paper for Printed Library Materials, ANSI Z39.48–1984.

CONTENTS

CONTENTS

INTRODUCTION

The Projected Trilogy

The drama of the *Sophist* is part of a continuing conversation. Three of its participants had talked the day before: Socrates who is known to the world as a philosopher, the brilliant young geometer Theaetetus who so uncannily resembles the ugly Socrates, and Theaetetus' elderly teacher Theodorus. A young friend of Theaetetus who shares not the looks but the name of the elder Socrates is a silent bystander in both conversations. In the earlier conversation, recounted in the dialogue *Theaetetus*, the young mathematician proves unsuccessful in his attempts to answer Socrates' question: What is knowledge? The dialogue ends with Socrates' urging his partners to resume their talk the following morning: for now Socrates must go off to answer the charges brought against him by Meletus, charges of impiety and corruption of the youth.

The conclusion of the *Theaetetus* leads us to expect another conversation between Theaetetus and Socrates the next day. Instead, as we see from the opening of the *Sophist*, something very different is about to take place. Theodorus has modified the terms of the appointment by bringing along a stranger, whom he recommends to Socrates as "a very philosophical man." Socrates seizes on the possibility that Theodorus has not recognized the stranger correctly: Perhaps he is a god in disguise! Theodorus brushes off this suggestion. The stranger is not a god, though he is godlike, for that is what he, Theodorus, calls all philosophers. By speaking so confidently—one might say, so unreflectively—of the stranger's philosophical nature, Theodorus unwittingly poses the question that will haunt the conversation: Who *is* the philosopher? Socrates intimates that true philosophers always appear in disguise, sometimes as statesmen, sometimes as sophists, while at other times they appear to be "in a totally manic condition." This last appearance drops out of sight. By calling attention to the possibility that Theodorus is deceived, Socrates has shifted the focus of yesterday's inquiry: the search for knowledge becomes the hunt for the purveyor of ignorance—the sophist.

The trinity sophist-statesman-philosopher suggests a triad of dialogues: *Sophist, Statesman, Philosopher*. We have the *Sophist* before us. The *Statesman* also exists, and its conversation takes place right after that of the *Sophist*. But there is no Platonic dialogue named the *Philosopher*. We are left to wonder:

Has the philosopher's nature already been implicitly revealed somewhere in the course of the two existing dialogues?

The Plot

In the prologue to the dialogue the stranger takes Theaetetus as a partner in the hunt for the sophist. To prepare for this difficult task, they first hunt down the fish-hunting angler. In this way the search for the sophist begins. (216A-221C).

I. *Getting.* The sophist turns up within five divisions of the getting art, the art of acquisition. Among other things, he is an angler-like hunter of rich kids, a sham virtue salesman, and a professional athlete in contests of words. (221C-226A).

II. *Separating.* The sophist is then found a sixth time as a practitioner of the homely art of separating, which includes spinning, combing and cleaning. In particular he is shown to be a philosopher-like cleanser of souls, who refutes others with a view to removing opinions that impede learning. (226A-231B).

III. *Making.* Confronted by what seems to be a disordered heap of possible determinations of the sophist, the stranger and Theaetetus decide to focus on one aspect of sophistry, the sophist as debater. Debating turns out to be a kind of making: the art of making spoken images of all things. This art of imitation has two forms: likeness-making and apparition-making, the making of true and of distorted images. But it is unclear in which division the sophist belongs. (231B-236D).

A. The very positing of an image-making art entails a number of difficulties; to articulate and resolve them is the task of the remainder of the dialogue. The existence of images presupposes that Non-being *is* . But Non-being appears to be unutterable, indeed, unthinkable. If the hunt for the sophist is to be brought to successful completion, the stranger and Theaetetus must find some way to say that Non-being *is* and Being *is not*—even if this involves committing a kind of intellectual parricide against the stranger's teacher, Parmenides. (236D-242B).

B. The turn to the question of Being occurs at the exact center of the dialogue. The stranger begins his inquiry into Being with a critical examination of claims men have made about it: He must show that Being is as difficult to come to terms with as Non-being. Six claims in all are shown to be wanting. The claim that Being is two and the Parmenidean claim that Being is one are dealt with first. The stranger then turns his dialectical powers against another pair, the giants who claim that everything that *is* is body and the gods who, ever at war with the giants, insist that only the invisible forms *are*. Out of the conflict emerges yet another claim about Being, which the stranger himself advances and then appears to demolish: Being is Motion and Rest together. The final claim about Being refuted by the stranger is that none of the kinds, including Being, mix together with any others. (242B-252C).

C. The stranger's critique of this last claim serves as the introduction to the dialogue's pivotal moment. The stranger and Theaetetus resolve to examine the ways in which the greatest of the kinds—Being, Rest and Motion—mix and do not mix together. But they no sooner begin their inquiry than they are forced to introduce two more kinds—the Same and the Other—and with this the solution to the problem of the sophist comes into view. For the Other is Non-being by another name, and it turns out to be the case, not only that the Other *is*, but that Being and beings participate in it and hence in some sense *are not*. (252C-259D).

D. What remains to be shown is that these conditions obtain in the case of speech, the medium of sophistry. The stranger and Theaetetus examine the structure of sentences as well as the relation of speech to opinion, thought and appearance in order to determine that and how Non-being makes its appearance within the realm of human speech and thinking. (259D-264B).

E. The stranger and Theaetetus are now able to track down the sophist a seventh time: within the class of apparition-making, i.e., the making of images that do not preserve the true proportions of their originals. The sophist is shown, among other things, to be a knowing imitator of what he does not know—a false image of the wise man rather than a true lover of wisdom. (264C-268D).

Real-Life Sophists and the Sophist's Kind

A fair-minded reader might wonder: Who in real life is the dark and wily operator that the stranger and Theaetetus are pursuing? There was in fact in the Greece of Socrates' time a tribe of travelling professors who gave themselves the honorific title "sophists," "wisdom-pliers," borrowed from the legendary Seven Sages of an earlier generation. Plato often brings them into his dialogues; the two most famous ones, Gorgias and Protagoras, have dialogues named after them, as do a number of minor sophists. When they appear in a dialogue, they are treated with real respect personally, though their activity, the selling of expertise, particularly of rhetorical techniques and of philosophical opinions, undergoes a politely devastating critique, usually unbeknownst to themselves.

In the *Sophist*, however, no particular, named sophist is under attack. Instead the stranger and Theaetetus investigate what in the nature of things makes such a being possible anywhere and at any time: In order to function profitably as a "trader of learnables" without quite knowing what he is doing, this persuasive expert in everything and nothing relies on the fact that nature is riddled with Non-being. Moreover the stranger allows it to appear that along certain lines the philosopher and sophist engage in like activities, though they diverge along others, as must an aspiring lover of wisdom diverge from a confident professor of wisdom. The sophist will appear as a universal expert, and the philosopher as a perpetual amateur of sorts. The sophist is the philosopher's lasting preoccupation, because he is, to a certain extent, a mirror image of the philosopher.

Father Parmenides

The figure who is in fact attacked by name in the dialogue and whose teachings undergo a devastating critique is, remarkably, the stranger's own teacher Parmenides. Parmenides was the first to inquire into Being and therefore might be thought of as the first philosopher, as the veritable father of philosophy. His insight into Being and Non-being was as follows: Being *is* and is the One and is the only thing that *is*, while Non-being is not even thinkable and ought not to be uttered.

Parmenides unveiled his insight in an epic poem, quoted three times in the *Sophist*. It begins as an account of the young Parmenides' blazingly grand initiation by a goddess into the heart of Being, and then sets out a "Way of Truth." Strangely enough, it also sets out a "Way of Opinion" (now lost)—strangely because opining is strictly impossible if only Being, along with its Truth, *is*.

As we are told in the Platonic dialogue that bears his name, Parmenides, with his associate Zeno, visited Athens when he was sixty-five and Socrates was a boy. Their conversation is set some time before the middle of the fifth century. Parmenides initiates young Socrates into the way of dialectic, the way of asking

THE SOPHIST'S THICKET (231D-E)

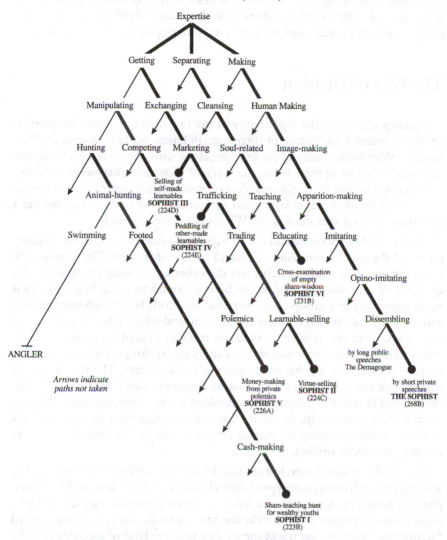

brief questions and refuting the answers; he generously uses his own One as the object of refutation. In the *Sophist*, which takes place over a half century later, Socrates slyly causes the reluctant stranger to employ a similar style.

In this dialogue, the stranger reluctantly commits philosophical parricide in pursuit of the sophist and his kind. If the sophist is not to have an impregnable hiding place in the impenetrable thicket of Non-being—a defense he gladly appropriates—Parmenides must be shown wrong in his principal insight, and Non-being must indeed be accessible to thought. It is part of the philosophical pathos of this inquiry that the elusive sophistic kind is merely netted, while the actual man who fathered philosophy is, as it were, done in.

The Way of Division

Socrates appears in the *Sophist* only in the beginning, to pose the question about the naming and nature of three human kinds: Sophist, Statesman, Philosopher. Why do Socrates and the stranger, along with docile young Theaetetus, care about the first of these types, the sophist? How does this pseudo-philosopher manage to give rise to this grandest of philosophical conversations? How is the Way of Division particularly good for pursuing the sophist? Can we call it a method? Does it seek definitions? What does it actually find?

In the world of Socrates and the stranger—the one a stay-at-home philosopher and the other a travelling one—and of Theodorus and Theaetetus—the one a seasoned old mathematician and the other a promising young one—the question of expertise, art, and know-how is bound to loom large, just as it might nowadays in a group of teachers and students. Which subjects are solid and which trivial? Which teachers are genuine and which fake? The pursuit of the sophist gives the stranger an occasion to chart human expertise—to show who gets things and who makes them (a shaky distinction, as our term "making money" shows), and in what mode and with what motive. The reader will see that part of the ensuing fun is that name-assigning subtly shades into name-calling, and that in this project no pretensions are honored, for louse-catching is parallel to generalship. In short, the stranger mounts a tongue-in-cheek critique of the inventory of human employments, while Socrates, we may imagine, stands by smiling.

Presumably Socrates is no less amused by the delineation of the sophist who, at several crucial points, comes perilously close to being the same as the philosopher. In particular, Expertise as a whole is rather surreptitiously divided into three parts—a proper division calls for two—and in this central part, called "separating," the stranger tracks the sophist into the kind of soul-cleansing by refutation of error that is usually attributed to Socrates. Thus the sophist is like the philosopher—at least as like as a wolf is to a dog, the stranger says.

So the sophist is represented as a sort of rogue philosopher, a wild beast that ranges over the chart of arts. What is this wildness of his? He runs away; he is a hunter who is himself to be hunted; he plunges deep into a thicket that seems pathless; he tricks his pursuers into a series of impasses, yet he himself runs all over within his thicket; he confuses the proper forkings of paths. Thus he turns up in many lairs—seven times, in fact. Not only does he have the expertise of *getting* money in bewilderingly different ways, he also *makes* everything—the whole world!—by his imitating art. Here, within the form of imitation, he is finally collected in the stranger's net—the genuine sophist, finally but surely not conclusively caught.

These trackings of the sophist give the stranger a chance to practice with Theaetetus and to show Socrates a brilliant working case of a way not entirely new to him (*Phaedrus* 266B), the way of making divisions and of collecting the results into a long descriptive name.

The way of division addresses the question "What is it?" by pursuing the question "Where is it?"; in this case the "it" is an activity requiring expertise. The way proceeds by cutting a given field into two, rejecting half, and attending to the other, and then again and again cutting the remainder in two, until the object sought is boxed into a small enough territory. Then all the names of the branches are collected, and a long descriptive title results. Sometimes the division is thought of as a left-hand and right-hand cut, and sometimes the slippery sophist has to be caught "with both hands," because he escapes into both sides of the cut at once. Sometimes, too, as if to undercut a false rigor in applying the method, a third division is slipped in, as was the case for the division of Expertise itself. The whole scheme, with all its aberrations, begs to be diagrammed not only in order to be seen clearly, but so as to invite reflection on the emphatically spatial character of this kind of thinking. That is why the reader is asked to inspect the diagram on page five.

A reader might get the impression that the actual divisions are comically redundant exercises and, moreover, are quite confused. They are, to be sure, sometimes hilarious spoofs of self-important professional titles. They are surely duplicative, but that is because the sophist is full of duplicity and never stays caught. One of them may indeed seem like a mere exercise, the one where the stranger and Theaetetus practice dividing by catching the angler (who, unlike his cousin, the sophist, once caught, stays hooked), though even these divisions bring to light something about division-making. But above all, the divisions are never pointlessly confused; even the dislocations are playfully subtle and suggestive.[1] Besides not being mere exercises, there are two more things the way of division is not—or is not yet. Although the Greek word for our term "way" is actually *methodos*, division here is not a full-blown "method of

---

[1] Here are two examples of apparently jumbled, but actually revealing passages. The first concerns the making of a division, the second the collection or recapitulation of a line of divisions.

    1. Sophist IV (see diagram) is ranged under "marketing," which is divided into self-selling of self-produced products and peddling of other people's products (224E). But in the summary of this division the stranger, with apparent carelessness, confuses levels and slips in a third case: the marketing and "trafficking" of things produced by oneself and by others. Since the Greek word for "self" is also

classification," a rigorously jigged procedure. Aristotle will apply division to the natural kinds of the animal kingdom and turn it into the method of classification by genera and species. But in the *Sophist* it is yet informal, tentative and fresh. It has not yet hardened into a confident but dry procedure.

Nor in the same vein is it yet a "method of definition," if we mean by defining producing a word-formula to match an already current word. In fact the participants invent words, "titles," to fit fields of activity never yet distinguished or named. And when Socrates had asked at the beginning about the "naming" of sophist, philosopher, statesman, it was not the terms as such he cared about but the human kinds behind them—whether they corresponded to the number of names.

And that is why the method, especially when applied to the sophist, serves the cause of philosophy so well. For who can help thinking beyond and behind the stranger's dividing activity to wonder what he must know beforehand to make his divisions and to catch the sophist who is all over the fields of expertise? Clearly the stranger must know—somehow or other—everything, just as the sophist claims to do. In particular, he must have some prior knowledge of the "kinds" and "forms" that give things their recognizable shape. In this dialogue we are not told how the stranger comes to recognize these ways the world has of sorting itself out. Instead the point is first somehow to locate these kinds and forms themselves and then, by way of division, to reveal and bring them to light—to make them explicit by marking them off. In this way the stranger lays the basis for understanding how the kinds or forms come to mix, to "interweave" with each other in a coherent and cohesive way.

All the divisions "specify" descents on the one hand and leave the lineage of the "other hand" indeterminate. On the diagram the light arrows pointing to nothing illustrate these indeterminacies. For each division that is pursued, another, with all its ramifications, is left in the dark; it leads into a disregarded

---

the word for "same," the stranger seems to confuse the divisions between stay-at-home peddling of things made by others and travelling sales of things made by oneself (Sophist III and IV on diagram), exemplifying that "interweaving" of Same and Other which will be a theme of the dialogue.

2. The dialogue ends with an apparently disordered collection of the sophist's titles, as one engaged in "making" (*poiesis*). They are said to be rewound like a skein from the last to the first (268C). (The sequence is visible on the right-hand line of the diagram.) Yet in the presentation of the final winding-up, the account is artfully deranged so as to place Imitation not merely in a middle but in a pivotal position. All the lower subdivisions that characterize the sophist as an opinionated dissembling argufier are represented as an *ascent* to the imitative division, while above it the sophist is shown as sharing with the poet one and the same *descent*, as he had before with the angler under "getting" and the philosopher under "separating." This crafty listing of the divisions not only shows once again how the kinds of Expertise are interwoven, but also that imitation, non-genuineness, marks the sophist in his very being.

thicket of possibilities. The very first division illustrates this point: Expertise is opposed to Non-expertise. Surely there is a lot more of the latter in the world, but we hear no more of it; it is entirely uncharted. For all we know, the sophist has escaped into these blank branchings as well, and there he remains entirely uncaught. Even farther into the background, though very much a floating presence in the dialogue, recedes the unifying title of Expertise and Non-expertise together: Power (*dynamis*).

Now these unbalanced dualities, one of which is definitely marked off while the other is left in indefinite opposition—consider the "infinite judgement" in later logic—imply a lurking presence that will become central to the dialogue: the Other. It turns out to be one of the "greatest kinds." For in these divisions the "other" fork leads not to a well-marked alternative—Amateur, for instance, would be a definite alternative to Expert—but just to Non-expert, a mere other, necessary for marking off the positive side but nevertheless merely a *non*-being. The discovery of Non-being as otherness, the deepest and most consequence-laden discovery of the *Sophist*, is thus foreshadowed by the way of division itself, though it is explicitly confronted only later, within one of the actual divisions, when the sophist is tracked into "image-making."

The Interweaving of Forms and Kinds

The way of division depends on the fact that we naturally and without much reflection discern forms and kinds. Every thing looks like other things and is recognized by us through the shape or form it has in common with them. We can hardly imagine coming across something that does not "look like" anything else at all. Thus any individual angler has the aspect or form (*eidos*) of Angler. But individual things are not alone in sharing a form. The forms themselves prove to be akin, to share a kindred nature and to belong to a more inclusive kind (*genos*). These higher forms or "greatest kinds" are introduced by the stranger not as "concepts," as objects formed by the mind, but rather as the most comprehensive beings that reveal themselves to us when we come to reflect on our speech about the way things are.

The most positive result of the stranger's parricide is the view that the forms or kinds are not radically separate from one another but constitute a community (*koinonia*). The stranger at one point provocatively refers to this community as an "interweaving of the forms." The image of weaving occurs regularly in the *Sophist*, although it is not until the *Statesman* that it replaces angling as the dominant image of the conversation. Weaving first comes up in the *Sophist* in the context of the stranger's hunt for the sophist within the kind he calls "separating." It is alluded to without being explicitly named. The descent into separating curiously reveals the sophist as a cross-examiner of empty sham-wisdom and therefore as entangled with the philosophic nature. Sophist and philosopher appear to be interwoven.

The image of weaving suggests that the interwoven elements retain their self-identity while being interrelated and incorporated into a greater whole. Such interweaving among the forms is the necessary condition for the possibility of all discourse. Discourse is the interweaving of names; and if this fabric or texture at the level of names were not somehow a reflection of the interweaving of beings, then speech and being would have nothing to do with one another. Philosophic inquiry would be impossible. Interweaving follows immediately from the identification of Non-being as otherness: The forms have the power of relating to one another, of participating in one another's natures, without sacrificing their distinctive identities. At the heart of all this community, participation and interweaving is the power of the Other. This is the power by which a being is what it is only by being other than *and therefore related* to everything else. With the interweaving of the forms, we come upon the power that distinguishes the philosophic nature from all others—the dialectical science that studies how a one wends its way through a many. For the second time in the dialogue, the hunt for the sophist, through the image of weaving, leads straight to the philosopher.

Images and Non-Being

The sophist's expertise appears in five comical yet ominous varieties within the kind of "getting," the acquisition of money and power through the purveying of sham-knowledge. In a sixth case, as a kind of "separating" that purifies the soul, this expertise achieves a dangerous dignity: sophistic refutation and Socratic questioning seem indistinguishable.

Even so, the sophist somehow remains uncaught. For this too can be said about him: He is, more than anything, a know-it-all, who has a "certain opinion-producing knowledge" about all things. The way to understand how a human being could know and display knowledge of everything is to see him as a maker of all things, a kind of artist of Being. Thus the sophist's art appears with a third lineage, that of "making," for which the Greek word is, conveniently, *poiesis,* "poetry." He is among those who mime things or paint them, or who make *images* in words.

But the sophist, we are told, will laugh at this all-out attempt to corner him. Taking advantage of Parmenides' teaching, he will claim that images have no place in the world. For they are curious hybrids. Here in the first analysis ever of the nature of an image we are shown that an image involves an interweaving of forms. Being and Non-being are intertwined in an image because in its very being an image is genuinely a likeness, though it is equally not what it pretends to be. It certainly *is* an image, but precisely as an image it *is not* the original. Anyone who paints the world in words is mixing Being with Non-being—including the philosopher.

But there are images and images. Some preserve the proportions of the original and are truthful likenesses; others are distortions—phantasms and apparitions of the original. The sophist is naturally identified as a producer of such apparitions. He is not only an image-maker, an "artist" in our sense—a dubious enough status—but he is something more and less: a con-artist. His facile duplications of the world are full of duplicity and shamming. He gives "phantastic" accounts and induces, for profit, deceptions and false opinions in the soul. Just as an admixture of Non-being makes possible that first fall from genuineness seen in images and imitations, so it is responsible for yet another second and further fall into positive falsity. To hold a false opinion is to think that what is not, *is* and what is, *is not*; to speak falsely is to say that what *is not* the case *is* the case and the reverse.

But again, the sophist will not stay cornered as a maker of false verbal images. He cunningly appeals to the great Parmenides himself, who had denied that exactly this was possible: to think and to say what *is not*. If the sophist is to be caught as a maker of counterfeit accounts, Father Parmenides must be gotten out of the way.

Non-Being as Otherness

The sophist as a kind can be grasped only if falsity is possible. But the False in things and in words, that which makes them pseudo-things and pseudo-accounts (*pseudos* being the Greek word for "falsehood"), is shot through with Non-being: Just as imitations *are not* what they seem to be, so false sentences say what *is not* the case. Now if Non-being is unthinkable and unutterable, as Father Parmenides asserted, then we may conclude that all speech must be granted to be true for those who utter it. Perfect relativity reigns.

Parmenides' dangerous single-mindedness cannot be overthrown by the mere counter-assertion of the paradox that Non-being after all somehow *is*. Non-being has to be given a meaning; it has to be rendered specific and placed among the articulable kinds. The stranger helps Theaetetus to discover the great and comprehensive kind that does indeed make Non-being sayable: the Other. When Non-being is specified as otherness, it becomes a powerful principle for regulating the slippery relativity that is the sophist's refuge.

The Other controls relativity in two ways. First it is itself the principle of relativity which turns the swampy *relativity* of "everything is true for someone" into a firm source of *relationality*. The Other does this work by being chopped up and distributed through all beings or, in the dialogue's other metaphor, by being thoroughly interwoven with Being. Every being, every thing, is not only the same with itself but also other than all the other beings. Each being is related to all the others by the reciprocating principle of otherness: It is the others' other without being the less itself, the less self-same.

So the Other acts as a sort of divisive bond that enables speech to mark off each kind or thing from all the others without consigning any of them to mere non-being or consigning itself to saying nothing. As the Other, Non-being does indeed become speakable. In fact the stranger's way of division relies continually on this power of the Other when it selects certain kinds and sets aside the other or non-selected kinds.

Non-being interpreted as the Other thus ceases to be mere nothingness and becomes instead the source of articulated diversity in things and in thought. Parmenides has been superseded.

But the sophist's relativity has not yet been completely controlled. The stranger has shown that Non-being, far from being unutterable, is in fact a necessary ingredient in thought and speech. To catch the sophist, however, another step is needed. The stranger does not just speak; he speaks falsehood, makes pseudo-arguments, offers imitation-wisdom. Though the Other is Non-being positively understood, it is still negative enough to help account not only for the diversity of kinds but also for differences in their dignity. An image or an imitation, because it has a share in Non-being, is not merely other than its original but also less. It is less in genuineness and may even fall further into falsity. The sophist can no longer claim that there is no intelligibile discrimination between true and false.

The Other as positive Non-being thus has a double function: First it establishes a world of diversity through which the multifarious sophist ranges, with the stranger in hot pursuit. And second, the Other plays a role in establishing the hierarchy of genuineness in which the sophist is caught and marked by the stranger as one who truly deals in falsity.

St. John's College, Annapolis
1995

A Note on Typography

We have tried to adhere to the following translational postulates: Our translation should be faithful to the Greek. Furthermore, Plato's Greek makes sense, and so should our English. The dialogue is a lively conversation whose mood and diction swing from stately to comical, and our translation should attempt to convey it at that. The characters has a range of formulaic replies that are nonetheless often very revealing and should be consistently rendered. The dialogue preserves the gestures and intonations of living languages by means of dozens of those little parts of speech called particles, and they should be rendered as faithfully as possible.

But above all we required that our translation of the most frequent and weighty words should be as unstrained and nontechnical as possible, preserving the still fresh root-meanings and suggestive connotations of a Greek vocabulary just on the brink of becoming fixed and philosophical in the technical sense.

We have had recourse to the following devices of typography and punctuation to convey meaning.

Italics are used for the verb *is* when it completes a sentence, as it may in Greek "Non-being *is*," which means "Non-being has being." This is a strange usage in English where "is" usually couples a subject and predicate. "Non-being *is* not contrary to Being but only other." One italicized *is* is often translated by others as "exists," but that verb has connotations of "being here and now" that are alien to this dialogue.

Capitals are used for the "greatest kinds," or "major forms," the most comprehensive terms of thought and speech; their presence in Greek is signalled by the definite article: "the Same", "the Other", "the Beautiful", "Being," too has an article in Greek, though it is not used in English.

Quotation marks are used at the first occurrence of an inverted use or a form of expertise, such as "pseudo-telling."

The pagination in the margin follows as closely as possible the standard one taken from the three-volume Plato edition of Henricus Stephanus, published in Paris in 1578.

A Note on Typography

We have tried to adhere to the following translators' postulates: Our translation should be faithful to the Greek. Furthermore, Plato's Greek makes sense, and so should our English. The dialogue is a lively conversation whose mood and diction swing from stately to comical, and our translation should attempt to convey that fact. Theaetetus has a range of formulaic replies that are nonetheless often very revealing and should be consistently rendered. The dialogue preserves the gestures and intonations of living languages by means of dozens of those little parts of speech called particles, and they should be rendered as faithfully as possible.

But above all we required that our translation of the most frequent and weighty words should be as unstrained and nontechnical as possible, preserving the still fresh root meanings and suggestive connotations of a Greek vocabulary just on the brink of becoming fixed and philosophical in the technical sense.

We have had recourse to the following devices of typography and punctuation to convey meaning:

Italics are used for the verb *is* when it completes a sentence, as it may in Greek: "Non-being *is*," which means "Non-being has being." This is a strange usage in English where "is" usually couples a subject and predicate: "Non-being is not contrary to Being but only other." Our italicized *is* often translated by others as "exists," but that verb has connotations of "being here and now" that are alien to this dialogue.

Capitals are used for the "greatest kinds" or "major forms," the most comprehensive terms of thought and speech; their presence in Greek is signalled by the definite article: "the Same," "the Other," "the Beautiful." "Being" too has an article in Greek, though it is not used in English.

Quotation marks are used at the first occurrence of an invented title for a form of expertise, such as "psycho-trading."

The pagination in the margin follows as closely as possible the standard one taken from the three-volume Plato edition of Henricus Stephanus, published in Paris in 1578.

The Sophist
or
The Professor of Wisdom

Theodorus

Socrates

Stranger from Elea

Theaetetus

216 A ***Theodorus:*** In accordance with yesterday's agreement, Socrates, we have duly come ourselves, and we're bringing along this stranger of sorts. His kin is from Elea, and he's an associate of the people around Parmenides and Zeno—a very philosophical man.

Socrates: Has it escaped your notice, Theodorus, that—by Homer's account—you're bringing not a stranger but some god? He says that
B besides the other gods the god of strangers especially becomes a companion to those men who participate in just reverence, and that he "looks down on both outrages and lawful conduct."[1] So perhaps here too some one of the higher powers may be accompanying you, to keep an eye on us and to refute us, since we are feeble at giving accounts—a sort of refuting god.

Theodorus: That, Socrates, is not the stranger's turn of mind; he's more measured than those who take polemics seriously. And to me
C the man seems to be in no way a god, though certainly godlike. For that's what I call all philosophers.

Socrates: Well said, my friend. But I'm afraid that this kind is not much easier to discern than that of "god." For certainly these men, abetted by the ignorance of others, make their appearance in all sorts of ways, roam about the cities and look down from on high at the life of those beneath—I don't mean the artificially philosophical but those who are so in their very being. To some people these men seem to be in no way honorable and to others in every way worthy,
D and sometimes they make their appearance as statesmen and some-

[1] *Odyssey* IX 269 ff; XVII 485 ff.

times as sophists, and sometimes they give the sense of being in a totally mad condition. I would, however, love to ask our stranger, if he likes, how the people who live over there tend to regard these things and what they've named them.

Theodorus: What things?

Socrates: Sophist, statesman, philosopher.

Theodorus: Since you're perplexed, what in particular and what sort of thing were you minded to ask about them?

Socrates: Just this: Are they accustomed to think that all these things are one or two, or do they divide them into three kinds—just as there are three names—and attach a kind to each one, name by name?

Theodorus: He won't, I suppose, begrudge you a run-through of these things. Or what should we say, stranger?

Stranger: Just what you did, Theodorus. I don't begrudge it at all, nor is it difficult to say that they generally consider them to be three. And yet, to mark off clearly what they are one by one is not a small nor an easy job.

Theodorus: It just so happens, Socrates, that you've gotten hold of arguments very close to those we happened to be questioning him about before we got here. What's more, he put us off then in just the way that he's now putting you off—after all, he admits he's certainly heard these things talked over enough and hasn't forgotten them.

Socrates: Well then, stranger, don't refuse us this first favor we've asked of you, but tell us only this much: Is it your preferred habit to go through whatever you wish to make clear to someone all by yourself in a long account? Or do you like to proceed through questioning? That's what Parmenides too once used—and he went through splendid accounts—when I was present as a young man and he at the time was very old.

Stranger: When the person to whom the conversation is addressed is unirritating and compliant, Socrates, the easier way to go through it is with another. If not, by oneself is easier.

Socrates: Well then, you can choose anyone you wish of those who are here. All of us will listen up meekly. Still, if you use me as advisor, you will choose one of the young men, this Theaetetus here or even one of the others, if that's more to your mind.

Stranger: Socrates, I feel a certain shame about making our first meeting together, not an exchange of brief words for words, but

instead a spinning out at great length of a long account by myself—
even if it's with another—as if I were making a display. For in truth
what must now be said is not what one might expect from the brev-
ity of the question; it happens to demand instead an account of
great length. And yet, not to do you and these others a favor appears to me to be ungracious and uncivilized, especially in light of
218 A what you've said. As for Theaetetus, I accept him wholeheartedly as
the one to converse with, both because of my earlier conversation
with him and because you now urge me to.

Theaetetus: But in that case, stranger, will you have done everyone
a favor by doing just as Socrates was saying?

Stranger: I'm afraid there's nothing more to be said along those
lines, Theaetetus. But beyond this point, the account, as it seems, is
likely to be addressed to you. And so, if you get weighed down by
the length of the labors, don't hold me responsible for it, but rather
these associates of yours.

B *Theaetetus:* But I really think I won't give up so soon. And in the
event that some such thing does happen, we'll take hold of Socrates
here as an ally. He has the same name as the other Socrates, but he's
my partner in age and in physical exercise, someone not unaccus-
tomed to working out with me in almost everything.

Stranger: Well spoken, and you'll take counsel about this with yourself as the account moves ahead. But in common with me you're
now to join the investigation, starting first, as it appears to me, from
C the sophist; and you're to search for and make apparent in speech
whatever he is. For right now you and I have only the name in
common about this fellow; but each of us may have, for ourselves,
his own private notion of the job we call by that name. But we must
always and about everything be in agreement with each other about
the thing itself through accounts rather than about the name alone
apart from an account. As for the tribe we're now intending to
search for—the sophist—it isn't the easiest of all things to gather
what it is. But it has been the opinion of everyone and from way
back that when it comes to great things that need to be well-elabo-
D rated, one must attend to them in small and easy matters first, before doing so in the very greatest. So now, Theaetetus, here's how I
at least counsel the pair of us: since we regard the sophist's kind as
difficult and hard to hunt down, to practice the way of inquiry first
on something else that's easier—that is, unless you from somewhere
or other can tell of another way that's more favorable.

Theaetetus: But I can't.

Stranger: Do you counsel, then, that we should go after something paltry and set it down as a model for the greater?

E *Theaetetus:* Yes.

Stranger: Then what could we put forth that's well-known and small but has no less an account than any of the greater things? Say, an angler. Isn't he both familiar to all and not worthy of much serious interest?

Theaetetus: Just so.

219 A *Stranger:* I do hope he offers us a way of inquiry and an account that's not unsuited to our purpose.

Theaetetus: That would be good.

Stranger: Come then, let us begin with him like this. And tell me: Shall we set him down as an expert or as some sort of non-expert, but having some other power?

Theaetetus: Least of all as a non-expert.

Stranger: But surely there are roughly two forms of all expertise?

Theaetetus: How so?

Stranger: Agriculture and the services dealing with every body subject to death, and then again what has to do with composite and
B artificial things (which we call equipment), and the imitative expertise as well—all these together would most justly be called by one name.

Theaetetus: How so and by what name?

Stranger: Regarding everything that someone might bring to beinghood—which *was not* before but afterwards *is*—we say, I suppose, that the bringer "makes" and the thing brought "is made."

Theaetetus: Correct.

Stranger: Now in fact all the kinds of expertise we just went through keep their power geared to this.

Theaetetus: That's what they do.

Stranger: So putting them under one heading, let us call them the "making art."

C *Theaetetus:* Let it be so.

Stranger: And again, after this, take the whole form of learning and that of getting to know, and take as well money-making and competing and hunting. Since none of them crafts anything, but instead in part manipulates, by speeches or deeds, whatever already *is* or has come to be, and in part refuses to be manipulated by others—surely for this reason, all these parts taken together would very appropriately be called a certain "getting art."

Theaetetus: Yes, that would be proper.

Stranger: Since getting and making comprise all the kinds of expertise

D taken together, in which of the two shall we put angling, Theaetetus?

Theaetetus: Clearly in getting, I suppose.

Stranger: But aren't there two forms of getting? One is the exchanging made by the willing with the willing through gifts and wages and purchases. And the remaining form, since it manipulates either by works or by speeches, would be, collectively, manipulative.

Theaetetus: That does appear from what's been said.

Stranger: Well, then, mustn't we cut "manipulating" in two?

Theaetetus: In which way?

Stranger: By setting down the whole out-in-the-open part as

E "competing" and all of it that's hidden as "hunting."

Theaetetus: Yes.

Stranger: Then surely it would be irrational not to cut hunting in two.

Theaetetus: Say how.

Stranger: By dividing it into hunting of the soulless kind and of the ensouled.

Theaetetus: Certainly, if in fact both *are.*

220 A *Stranger:* Surely both *are.* And besides, we must bid farewell to the one—the hunting of soulless things (unnamed except for certain parts of the diving art and other such trifling things)—and must call the other part, the hunting of ensouled animals, "animal-hunting."

Theaetetus: Let it be so.

Stranger: But might one not speak with justice of a double form of animal-hunting: that of the footed kind (itself divided into many forms and names), namely, "footed-animal-hunting" and the other, of the swimming animal, namely, "wetlands-animal-hunting" as a whole?

Theaetetus: Entirely so.

B *Stranger:* And of what swims we see one tribe that's winged and another that lives in the water?

Theaetetus: Of course.

Stranger: Then surely the whole hunt for the winged kind is said, I suppose, to be a sort of "fowling."

Theaetetus: So they say.

Stranger: And nearly the whole hunt for what lives in water is called "fishing."

Theaetetus: Yes.

Stranger: What about this: May I not in turn divide this hunt into its two greatest parts?

Theaetetus: Into what parts?

Stranger: The one conducts the hunt by using enclosures on the spot, the other by striking.

Theaetetus: How do you mean this? And in what way do you distinguish each of the two?

C   *Stranger:* In the one case, I mean that it seems right to give the name "enclosure" to anything that closes something off by surrounding it for the sake of obstruction.

Theaetetus: By all means.

Stranger: Then must we call fishing baskets and nets and snares and hoops and such things anything other than enclosures?

Theaetetus: Nothing else.

Stranger: Then this part of the chase we'll declare to be "enclosure-hunting" or some such thing.

Theaetetus: Yes.

Stranger: But what's accomplished by getting a strike with hooks and tridents is other than this, and we must now call it, in one word, a certain

D   "striking" hunt. Or could someone say it better, Theaetetus?

Theaetetus: Let's not worry about the name. This one will do.

Stranger: Well then, I suppose the nocturnal part of striking, which takes place by firelight, happens to be called "fire-hunting" by the very men who busy themselves with the hunt.

Theaetetus: Entirely so.

Stranger: But all of the daytime part is said to be "hook-hunting," since tridents too are tipped with hooks.

E   *Theaetetus:* So they say.

Stranger: Well then, the part of the hook-hunting part of the striking art that proceeds from on high to the depths—because it employs tridents most of all—is, I suppose, called "tridentry."

Theaetetus: Some at least assert this.

Stranger: But there remains, as it were, only one form more.

Theaetetus: What is it?

Stranger: The form of striking contrary to this. It is generated by means of a hook—with which someone would hit every single time, not any chance part of the body of the fishes, as with tridents, but only around the head and the mouth of the catch—and it pulls up from below in the contrary direction by means of sticks and reeds. What shall we say, Theaetetus, is the name by which this form must be designated?

Theaetetus: In my opinion at least, the very thing we recently proposed as necessary to find out has now been brought to an end.

Stranger: Now therefore, regarding angling, both you and I have not only reached agreement about the name, but have also gotten a sufficient hold on the account of the job itself. For of expertise as a whole, half was the getting part, and of getting, half was the manipulating, and of the manipulating, half was the hunting, and of hunting, half was the animal-hunting, and of animal-hunting, half was the wetlands-animal-hunting, and of wetlands-animal-hunting, the section below was as a whole the fishing part, and half of fishing was the striking, and half of striking was the hook-hunting; and half of this, the half that had to do with a strike pulled up from below— from which very action its name was copied—has turned out to be what we were searching for just now: "angling" by name.

Theaetetus: In every way this has been made sufficiently clear.

Stranger: Come then, in accordance with this model, let's try to find the sophist too, whatever he is.

Theaetetus: Exactly.

Stranger: And yet this was our first query about the angler—whether he was to be set down as a layman or as someone having some expertise.

Theaetetus: Yes.

Stranger: And now, shall we set down this other fellow, Theaetetus, as a layman or as truly in every way a "professor of wisdom?"

Theaetetus: In no way is he a layman. For I do understand what you mean: that he's far from being "wise" and yet does have this name.

Stranger: So, as it seems, he must be set down by us as having some expertise.

Theaetetus: Then what in the world is this expertise?

Stranger: By the gods, have we failed to notice that the one man is akin to the other?

Theaetetus: Who is akin to whom?

Stranger: The angler to the sophist.

Theaetetus: In what way?

Stranger: To me they both clearly appear as hunters of some sort.

E *Theaetetus:* What does this one hunt? For we spoke about the other.

Stranger: I suppose we divided the entire chase in two just now, cutting it into the swimming part and the footed.

Theaetetus: Yes.

Stranger: And we went through the one, in so far as it concerns swimming animals that live in the water; but the footed we let go uncloven, saying that it was multiform.

222 A *Theaetetus:* Entirely so.

Stranger: Now then, up to this point the sophist and the angler make their way as a pair, starting from the getting art.

Theaetetus: They do seem to.

Stranger: But they veer off at animal-hunting, where one turns, I suppose, towards the sea and the rivers and lakes to hunt the animals that live there.

Theaetetus: Certainly.

Stranger: And the other veers towards the land, towards certain other rivers of wealth and youth—unstinting meadows, as it were—where he means to manipulate the nurslings that live there.

B *Theaetetus:* What do you mean?

Stranger: The hunt on foot yields a certain pair of greatest parts.

Theaetetus: Each of which is?

Stranger: One part for the hunt of tame things, the other of wild.

Theaetetus: Then is there a hunt of tame things?

Stranger: If man is a tame animal. But put it in any way you like, whether you set down no animal as tame, or some other animal as tame but man as wild, or again, whether you say that man is tame but you consider there to be no hunt for men—whichever of these ways of saying it you consider congenial, mark off that one for us.

C *Theaetetus:* But, stranger, I do consider us to be a tame animal, and I say there's a hunt for men.

Stranger: Let us then say that "tame-hunting" is twofold.

Theaetetus: On what basis are we saying that?

Stranger: We mark off pirating and kidnapping and tyrannizing and the entire martial expertise as all one "forcible" hunt.

Theaetetus: Beautiful.

Stranger: And we call litigation and public speaking and socializing—again taking the thing as a whole—some one "credibility-producing" D expertise.

Theaeteus: Correct.

Stranger: So let us say that there are two kinds of credibility-producing.

Theaetetus: What are they?

Stranger: One arises in private, the other in public.

Theaetetus: Each form certainly does arise.

Stranger: Again, isn't it the case that of "private-hunting" one part is "pay-earning," the other "gift-bearing?"

Theaetetus: I don't understand.

Stranger: It seems you haven't yet put your mind to the hunt of lovers.

Theaetetus: What about it?

E *Stranger:* That on top of everything else they give gifts to those they hunt.

Theaetetus: What you say is very true.

Stranger: So then let this form be that of "erotic expertise."

Theaetetus: Entirely so.

Stranger: But the part of the pay-earning expertise that socializes through gratification and has done its hooking entirely through pleasure and that only demands sustenance as its pay—we would all say, as I think, that it is a "flattering," a certain "pleasuring expertise."

223 A *Theaetetus:* Of course.

Stranger: But the part which professes to socialize for the sake of virtue yet demands cold cash as its pay—isn't this kind worthy of being called by another name?

Theaetetus: Of course.

Stranger: So what is this name? Try to say.

Theaetetus: It's clear. For we seem to me to have discovered the sophist. At any rate, in saying this, I'd think I was calling him by the name that fits.

B *Stranger:* According to the present account, Theaetetus, it seems that what belongs to the appropriating, hunting, animal-hunting, land-lubbing, human-hunting, private-hunting, cash-making, sham-teaching expertise—amounting to a hunt for wealthy and well-known youths—must be called, so our present account concludes, "sophistry."

Theaetetus: That's altogether so.

Stranger: But let's look at it in this way as well. For the object of our
C present search participates in no plain expertise but in a very complex one. Why, even in what was said earlier, it offers the appearance of being not what we're now claiming it is, but some other kind.

Theaetetus: How so?

Stranger: The form of the getting expertise was somehow double: it had a hunting part and also an exchanging part.

Theaetetus: It certainly did.

Stranger: Well then, should we say there are two forms of the exchanging expertise, one "gift-giving," the other "marketing?"

Theaetetus: Let this be said.

Stranger: And we shall in turn claim that marketing is cut in two.

D *Theaetetus:* In what way?

Stranger: By distinguishing between the "self-selling" of self-produced products and "trafficking," which traffics in the products of others.

Theaetetus: Entirely so.

Stranger: What about this: In the case of trafficking, isn't exchange within the city—which is roughly the half part of it—called "peddling?"

Theaetetus: Yes.

Stranger: But that part which carries on exchange from one city to another by buying and selling is called "trading?"

Theaetetus: Certainly.

Stranger: In the case of trading, don't we perceive that one part
E exchanges by selling for cash just those things by which the body is nourished and which it uses, while the other part does the same for the soul?

Theaetetus: What do you mean by this?

Stranger: No doubt we're ignorant of the part that concerns the soul, since we do, I suppose, understand the other.

Theaetetus: Yes.

224 A *Stranger:* Then as for culture as a whole, along with painting and wonder-working and many other soul-related things that are carried and traded, some for diversion and others for a serious purpose: Since it constantly goes from city to city, bought in one place and carried to

another and sold, it confers on its carrier and seller the designation "trader" not a jot less correctly than does the sale of food and drink.

Theaetetus: What you say is most true.

B *Stranger:* Then will you also apply the same name to the man who buys up learnables and passes them on for cash into one city and out of another?

Theaetetus: Definitely.

Stranger: Then wouldn't part of this "psycho-trading" most justly be called "displaying?" And as for the other part—which is no less ridiculous than the first—since it is nevertheless the selling of learnables, isn't it necessary to call it by some name that's germane to the business?

Theaetetus: By all means.

Stranger: Well then, with respect to this "learnable-selling," the
C part that has to do with the learnables of the other arts should be called by one name, the part that has to do with the virtue-related learnable by another.

Theaetetus: Of course.

Stranger: "Techno-selling" might be just the name to harmonize with the part that concerns the other learnables. But you put your heart into it and say the name of the one who sells virtue.

Theaetetus: And what other name might someone utter without hitting a false note except to say that it's what we're searching for right now—the sophistic kind?

Stranger: None other. So come then, let us now gather it all together by saying that, as the part of getting, of trafficking, of marketing, of
D trading, of psycho-trading—which part has to do with speeches and learnables and sells virtue—there has come to light for a second time: sophistry.

Theaetetus: Very much so.

Stranger: But take a third case: If someone who settled down in a city to sell some learnables while concocting others himself, sold these same learnables and set out to make his living from this, I for one think you would call it by no other name than the one you used just now.

Theaetetus: And why shouldn't I?

Stranger: Then also the trafficking part of getting, the marketing
E part, taken in both ways, whether as peddling or as self-selling—whichever the learnable-selling kind is that has to do with the things we mentioned—you, apparently, will always call "sophistic."

Theaetetus: It's a necessity. For one must follow along with the account.

Stranger: Then let's keep a further lookout to see whether the kind we're now in hot pursuit of is like this sort of thing.

225 A *Theaetetus:* What thing?

Stranger: Competing was for us a part of getting.

Theaetetus: It was, in fact.

Stranger: There is therefore nothing out of the way in dividing it in two.

Theaetetus: Say how.

Stranger: By setting down one part of this expertise as "contending" and the other part as "battling."

Theaetetus: That's it.

Stranger: Then it's fairly likely and proper for us to give the battling part that pits body against bodies some such name as the following and set it down as "doing violence."

Theaetetus: Yes.

Stranger: And the part that pits words against words, Theaetetus—
B would one call it anything else except "disputing?"

Theaetetus: Nothing else.

Stranger: And surely the part concerning disputes must also be set down as twofold.

Theaetetus: How?

Stranger: Insofar as it is generated in public by reams against opposing reams of arguments and has to do with just and unjust acts, it is "pleading."

Theaetetus: Yes.

Stranger: And again, do we customarily call the part that takes place in private and is all chopped up by questions pitted against answers anything but "debating?"

Theaetetus: Nothing but.

Stranger: And let so much of debating as disputes about contracts and
C is practiced randomly and amateurishly be posited as a form, since the account has discerned it as distinct. It hasn't, however, gotten a title from our predecessors, nor does it deserve one from us now.

Theaetetus: True, because it is divided into parts too small and of every which sort.

Stranger: And again, don't we customarily call the highly expert part that disputes both about the just things themselves and about unjust things and about all the rest "polemics?"

Theaetetus: Of course.

D   *Stranger:* Well then, of the polemical part one part happens to waste money and the other to make it.

Theaetetus: Altogether so.

Stranger: Let us then try to say the title by which we must call each of these.

Theaetetus: Indeed we must.

Stranger: Now it seems to me that the part which becomes careless of its own affairs because of the pleasure of passing the time in this way, but which is not listened to with equal pleasure by most of those who do listen, because of its style—in my own view it is to be called nothing other than "yammering."

Theaetetus: For that's about what they say.

E   *Stranger:* As for its contrary, then, which makes money from private polemics, you in turn now try to say its name.

Theaetetus: And what else could someone say and not miss the mark except that here, once again and now for the fourth time, there has arrived that wondrous object of our hot pursuit, the sophist?

226 A *Stranger:* It seems that the money-making kind, which belongs to the polemical, the debating, the disputing, the battling, the competing, the getting art, is, as the account has just disclosed, nothing but—the sophist.

Theaetetus: Exactly.

Stranger: You see, then, how true it is to say that this beast is complex and, as the saying goes, not to be grabbed with one hand or the other.

Theaetetus: Then we must grab him with both.

Stranger: We must indeed, and we must do it as best we can by
B pursuing this track of his. Tell me: I take it that we employ in public some of the names our domestics use?

Theaetetus: Yes, many. But which of these many names are you inquiring about?

Stranger: These: for example, we speak of "straining" and "sifting" and "winnowing" and "separating."

Theaetetus: Certainly.

Stranger: What's more, in addition to these, we know that "carding, "spinning," "combing," and thousands of other such things are involved in the arts. Isn't that true?

C   *Theaetetus:* Why do you keep bringing up these examples and asking about them all? What do you wish to make clear about them?

Stranger: I suppose the things mentioned are all said to be ways of dividing.

Theaetetus: Yes.

Stranger: Well then, according to my account, on the assumption that in these matters there's one expertise in all, we'll think it worthy of one name.

Theaetetus: What'll we call it?

Stranger: The "separating" art.

Theaetetus: So be it.

Stranger: Then look to see where in turn we'd be able to catch sight of two forms of this.

Theaetetus: You're ordering me to do some quick looking.

D   *Stranger:* And yet, in the separations mentioned earlier there was the removing of worse from better and also that of like from like.

Theaetetus: What was said just now makes that fairly clear.

Stranger: Well then, for the one I don't have a name in common use. But for the separating that leaves behind the better and casts off the worse, I do have a name.

Theaetetus: Say what it is.

Stranger: As I see it, every separating of this sort is said by everybody to be a means of cleansing.

Theaetetus: It's said to be.

E   *Stranger:* Then would not everyone see the "cleansing" form in turn as double?

Theaetetus: Well yes, maybe at their leisure they would. I, however, don't see it now.

Stranger: And yet, it's fitting that the many forms of body-related cleansings be comprehended by one name.

Theaetetus: What forms and by what name?

Stranger: There are the cleansings of living beings, which deal with
227   A   whatever's cleansed inside their bodies and is rightly separated out by gymnastics and doctoring, and also whatever's on the outside, things trivial to mention, which are provided for by the bath attendant's art. And then there are the cleansings of soulless bodies, whose care is provided for by brushing and the whole art of decorating. This, with

its minutiae, has gotten many names that seem ridiculous.

Theaetetus: Very.

Stranger: Altogether ridiculous, Theaetetus. But as a matter of fact, the Way of Accounts happens to care neither more nor less for sponging than for drinking medicine, for whether the one type of cleansing

B benefits us a little or the other a lot. The reason is that, in trying to understand—for the sake of getting insight—what is akin and not akin in all the arts, it honors them all equally and does not, in making its comparisons, consider some any more ridiculous than others; nor has it ever regarded the one who clarifies hunting through the general's art as any more awesome than one who does so through louse-catching but only, for the most part, as more vain. And now, as for the very thing you were asking about—what name we shall give to all the powers whose lot it is to cleanse either the ensouled or the soulless body—it will make no difference at all to the Way

C what sort of term will seem most becoming. Only let the term have the ability to bind together all the cleansings of other things, while keeping separate the cleansings of the soul. For the Way has just now been trying to mark off the cleansing that concerns thinking from the others—if, that is, we understand exactly what it intends.

Theaetetus: I *have* understood: I grant that there are two forms of cleansing, and that one form has to do with the soul and is separate from the form that has to do with the body.

Stranger: Most beautifully done. Now as for what comes next, listen

D to me and try again to cut the term in two.

Theaetetus: In whatever way you lead, I'll try to cut along with you.

Stranger: Do we say that in the soul villainy is something other than virtue?

Theaetetus: Of course.

Stranger: And cleansing was the leaving alone of that but the throwing out of whatever's base anywhere.

Theaetetus: Yes, it was.

Stranger: Moreover, with respect to the soul, to the extent that we discover some taking away of the bad, we shall sound in tune if we call it a cleansing.

Theaetetus: Very much so.

Stranger: Surely we must say that there are two forms of badness pertaining to the soul.

Theaetetus: What are they?

228   A *Stranger:* The one is like sickness that arises in the body, the other like ugliness.

Theaetetus: I don't understand.

Stranger: Perhaps you've never regarded sickness and sedition as the same thing?

Theaetetus: I don't know what I ought to answer to this either.

Stranger: Do you consider sedition to be anything but the differing of what is by nature akin, arising from some sort of dissolution?

Theaetetus: Nothing else.

Stranger: But is ugliness anything but that everywhere ill-formed kind, "lack of measure"?

  B *Theaetetus:* Nothing but.

Stranger: Well then, don't we perceive that the following elements carry on their differences in the soul of those who are in a condition of baseness: opinions with desires, and spiritedness with pleasures, and reason with pains, and all such things with one another?

Theaetetus: Definitely.

Stranger: Yet all of them must necessarily be closely akin.

Theaetetus: Of course.

Stranger: And so we'll speak correctly if we say that villainy is sedition and sickness of the soul.

Theaetetus: Very correctly.

  C *Stranger:* What about this: When things that participate in motion put forth some goal and try to achieve it, and at each attempt are deflected from it and fail to achieve it, shall we say that they're liable to this because there's a common measure that they have among them or, on the contrary, because of lack of measure?

Theaetetus: Clearly because of lack of measure.

Stranger: But of course we know that every soul that is ignorant of anything is so unwillingly.

Theaetetus: Definitely.

  D *Stranger:* Now being ignorant—when the soul makes an attempt at the truth but the intelligence becomes deflected—is nothing else than mental derangement.

Theaetetus: By all means.

Stranger: Then the mindless soul must be set down as ugly and lacking measure.

Theaetetus: It seems so.

Stranger: And so there are, as it appears, these two kinds of bad within the soul. The one is called villainy by most people and is very clearly a sickness of soul.

Theaetetus: Yes.

Stranger: And the other they call ignorance; but when it comes about only inside the soul, they aren't willing to agree that it's badness.

E *Theaetetus:* What I had doubts about when you said it just now, must absolutely be granted—that there are two kinds of badness in the soul, and also that cowardice and unrestraint and injustice must altogether be considered a sickness in us, while the condition of multiple and manifold ignorance must be set down as ugliness.

Stranger: Then isn't it the case that for the body there has arisen a certain pair of arts to deal with this pair of conditions?

Theaetetus: What pair of arts?

229 A *Stranger:* For ugliness there's "physical training," for disease, "doctoring."

Theaetetus: That's apparent.

Stranger: Then also for insolence and injustice and cowardice, isn't "disciplining," of all the arts, the one closest in nature to justice?

Theaetetus: That's likely, at least as far as human opinion goes.

Stranger: What about this: For ignorance as a whole, would there be any expertise one would more correctly name than "teaching?"

Theaetetus: None.

Stranger: Come then. Look to see whether we must declare that there
B is only one kind of teaching—or else more with two greatest parts.

Theaetetus: I'm looking.

Stranger: It seems to me that we'd find out fastest in this way.

Theaetetus: In what way?

Stranger: By looking to see if ignorance has some cut somewhere along its middle. For if ignorance turns out to be twofold, it's clear that it will compel teaching to have two parts as well, one for each one of its kinds.

Theaetetus: Well, is the object of our present search clear to you in some way?

C *Stranger:* At least I think I see a great and grievous form of ignorance that's marked off from the rest and equal in weight to all its other parts.

Theaetetus: What is it?

Stranger: Having the opinion that one knows something while not really knowing it—through this seem to arise all the many ways in which we are tripped up in thought.

Theaetetus: True.

Stranger: What's more, I suppose that to this form of ignorance alone the name "lack of learning" is applied?

Theaetetus: Entirely so.

Stranger: And what name, then, must we give to the part of teaching that removes it?

D   *Theaetetus:* I imagine, stranger, that the other part has been called "vocational training," while around here the latter part has been called, through our influence, "education."

Stranger: Indeed it has been called this, Theaetetus, among nearly all the Greeks. But we must look at education too to see whether it is, as a whole, uncut or has some division worthy of a title.

Theaetetus: We must certainly look.

Stranger: Well then, it seems to me that this too is split somewhere.

Theaetetus: Along what lines?

Stranger: Of the teaching that takes place in speeches, one way
E   seems to be rougher, the other smoother.

Theaetetus: What should we call each of them?

Stranger: One is the time-honored way of our fathers, which they used to employ and many still employ toward their sons, whenever they go
230 A astray in some way—sometimes being harsh with them and sometimes exhorting them more gently. This, as a whole, one would speak of most correctly as "admonishing."

Theaetetus: Just so.

Stranger: On the other hand, some, after giving themselves an account, seem to consider that all lack of learning is involuntary, and that the man who thinks he's wise isn't at all willing to learn those things about which he thinks he's terrific, and that the admonishing form of education accomplishes little with a lot of toil.

Theaetetus: And they believe rightly.

B *Stranger:* So they embark on the expulsion of this opinion in another manner.

Theaetetus: What manner?

Stranger: They question someone on those topics about which he thinks he's saying something when in fact he's saying nothing. Then, inasmuch as the people they question wander in their opinions, they easily inspect them; and bringing those opinions together in the same place through discussion, they put them alongside each other and, by putting them together in this way, display the opinions as contradicting themselves about the same things with respect to the same points in C the same ways. And those who see this are harsh with themselves and tame towards others, and this is precisely the manner in which they are delivered from their big and stiff opinions about themselves. Of all deliverances this one is the most pleasant to listen to and for the man who suffers it the one that takes the firmest hold. The reason, my dear boy, is that just as doctors who tend bodies have always believed that a body would not be able to derive benefit from the food it's offered until someone casts out the impediments in it, so too, those who cleanse the people we've just mentioned, sharing the doctors' belief, have had the same thing in mind about the soul: It will have no profit from the D learning it's offered until someone, by refuting and putting to shame the one refuted and by taking out the opinions that impede learning, renders him clean and makes him consider himself as knowing only what he knows and no more.

Theaetetus: Certainly that's the best and most sound-minded condition.

E *Stranger:* For all these reasons, Theaetetus, we must say that refutation is the greatest and lordliest of cleansings; and we must believe that the man who is unrefuted—even if he happens to be the Great King—since he's uncleansed in the greatest matters, has turned out uneducated and deformed in those things in which it was fitting to be most clean and beautiful for the man who was to be genuinely happy.[2]

Theaetetus: That's altogether so.

Stranger: But what about this: Who shall we say are the practitioners 231 A of this expertise? I'm afraid to say sophists.

Theaetetus: Why?

Stranger: So as not to confer on them too great an honor.

Theaetetus: And yet the description just given is like someone of that sort.

Stranger: And so is a wolf like a dog—the wildest like the tamest. But to be safe, one must be on one's guard about similarities more than anything—their kind is extremely slippery. Just the same, let them stand as sophists. For whenever people are sufficiently on their

---

[2] The "Great King" is the king of Persia, Artaxerxes II at the time of this conversation, 399 B. C., the year of Socrates' execution.

B   guard, I think the later dispute will arise over no minor boundaries.

Theaetetus: At least it's not likely.

Stranger: Then let cleansing belong to the separating expertise, and from cleansing let the soul-related part be marked off, and from this, teaching, and from teaching, education. And of education let the cross-examination that arises concerning empty sham-wisdom be called, in the account that has just appeared, nothing else but the bred-to-kind kind of *sophistry.*

C   *Theaetetus:* Let it be so called. But for my part, since he's already appeared to be so many things, I'm now at an impasse as to what in the world we must say the sophist is in his very being, if I'm to tell the truth and affirm it confidently.

Stranger: Your being at an impasse is likely enough. But then we must consider that he too is by now totally at an impasse about how he'll continue to slip through our account. For the wrestlers' proverb is right: "Not easy to escape all the holds." So now we must really go after him.

Theaetetus: Beautifully said.

Stranger: First then, let's stop so as to catch our breath, and while
D   resting let's reckon up for ourselves in how many ways the sophist has appeared to us. For in my opinion he was first found to be a paid hunter of the young and the rich.

Theaetetus: Yes.

Stranger: And second, a kind of trader in soul-related learnables.

Theaetetus: Entirely so.

Stranger: And third, didn't he show up as a peddler of the same things?

Theaetetus: Yes, and fourth, he showed up for us as a self-seller of learnables.

Stranger: You remembered correctly. But I will try to remember
E   the fifth. For he was a kind of athlete practiced in argument-competition who marked off as his own the polemical expertise.

Theaetetus: He was indeed.

Stranger: The sixth, then, was disputable, but just the same, we granted him this: to be set down as a soul-related cleanser of opinions that impede learning.

Theaetetus: That's altogether so.

232   A   *Stranger:* Do you see, then, that whenever someone appears to be a knower of many things and yet is called by the name of one expertise,

there's something unsound about this appearance? Indeed, isn't it clear that when a person experiences this with respect to some expertise, he's not able to see what all these studies have in view—and that's why he calls their possessor by many names instead of one?

Theaetetus: It seems to crop up like this most of the time.

B *Stranger:* Well then, let's avoid experiencing this in our search because of laziness. Instead, let's begin by taking up again something that was said about the sophist. For it's apparent to me that one thing reveals him most of all.

Theaetetus: What's that?

Stranger: At some point we claimed he was a debater.

Theaetetus: Yes.

Stranger: What about this: Didn't we also claim that he becomes a teacher of this very thing to others?

Theaetetus: Certainly.

C *Stranger:* Then we should look at what such men claim to make others debaters about. Let's begin looking in this way. Come, do they make men competent to debate about those divine things which are not apparent to most men?

Theaetetus: At least that's said about them.

Stranger: And about what's apparent on earth and in the heavens and the like?

Theaetetus: Certainly.

Stranger: Moreover, in private get-togethers, whenever there's talk about the becoming and beinghood of all things, we know that they themselves are terrific at debating and that they make others able to debate in these very matters?

Theaetetus: Altogether so.

D *Stranger:* And don't they promise as well to make men able to dispute about laws and political affairs as a whole?

Theaetetus: Why, virtually no one would converse with them if they didn't promise this.

Stranger: Moreover, the things pertaining to all the arts and to each single art—about which the craftsman himself must debate with each man—have been set down in writing and published for anyone who wants to learn.

Theaetetus: It appears to me that you've described the Protagorean
E texts about wrestling and the other arts.[2]

---

[2] Protagoras lived in the generation between Parmenides and Socrates. In

Stranger: And many others, bless you! But regarding the debating expertise, does it seem, in sum, to be a power adequate to disputing about all things?

Theaetetus: At any rate, it appears to leave almost nothing out.

Stranger: By the gods, my boy, do you think this is possible? For perhaps you young men may see this more acutely, while we see it more dimly.

233 A *Theaetetus:* What do you mean? And what in particular are you referring to? I don't yet see what's being asked right now.

Stranger: I'm asking whether it's possible for any human being to know all things.

Theaetetus: Blessed indeed would our kind be, stranger, if it were possible!

Stranger: Then how could someone who is himself a non-knower ever be able to say anything sound in debating with one who knows?

Theaetetus: There's no way.

Stranger: So what in the world could the wondrous sophistic power be?

Theaetetus: Wondrous in what respect?

B *Stranger:* The way they have of being able to equip young men with the opinion that they themselves are in all things the wisest of all. For it's clear that if they neither debated correctly nor appeared to do so to those young men, or again, if in appearing to debate correctly they didn't seem thoughtful through their disputing, hardly anyone—to quote you—would have wanted to give them money to become their student in these same matters.

Theaetetus: Hardly anyone, to be sure.

Stranger: But now, do people in fact want to?

Theaetetus: Very much so.

C *Stranger:* The reason, I suppose, is that they themselves seem to be in a knowledgeable condition regarding those very things they debate about.

the dialogue *Protagoras* Plato makes him say that unlike other sophists who try to disguise themselves, he grants that he is indeed a sophist and that he educates people (317 B). Among his writings was a large treatise called *Counterarguments* or *Debates* (*Antilogiai*) which contained, along with parts on the gods and on Being, articles on the various kinds of expertise, among them one article entitled "On Wrestling." The Greek verb connected with *Antilogiai, antilegein,* "to counterargue" or "to talk against," which we translate "to debate," abounds in this section.

Theaetetus: Of course.

Stranger: And they bring this off, we're saying, regarding all things?

Theaetetus: Yes.

Stranger: Then in all things they appear wise to their students.

Theaetetus: Certainly.

Stranger: Although they aren't, for that was shown to be impossible.

Theaetetus: Of course it's impossible.

Stranger: Then the sophist—the professor of wisdom—has come to light as someone who has a certain opinion-producing knowledge about all things, but not true knowledge.

D *Theaetetus:* That's altogether so, and what was said just now is very likely the most correct thing said about them yet.

Stranger: In that case, let's get hold of some clearer model in these matters.

Theaetetus: What model?

Stranger: This one—and try to put your mind to answering really well.

Theaetetus: What are you asking?

Stranger: Whether someone might claim that he knew not how to speak nor how to debate but how to make and do all things by virtue of one expertise.

E *Theaetetus:* How do you mean "all"?

Stranger: Why, your ignorance goes right back to the beginning of what we said. For you seem not to understand "all things."

Theaetetus: I *don't.*

Stranger: In that case, I mean you and me among "all things" and, besides us, the other animals and the trees.

Theaetetus: What are you getting at?

Stranger: Whether someone might claim that he'll make me and you and all other things that grow.

234 A *Theaetetus:* Meaning what exactly by "making"? For surely you don't mean some sort of farmer, since you said he was also a maker of animals.

Stranger: Yes, and what's more, of the sea and the earth and the heavens and the gods and all other things. And furthermore, after he's quickly made each of them, he sells them off for very small change.

Theaetetus: You're playing some joke!

Stranger: Really? Don't we have to regard it as a joke when someone says that he knows everything and would teach it to another for a little money and in a little time?

Theaetetus: Entirely so, I suppose.

B *Stranger:* And do you know a more artful or delightful form of joke than the imitative one?

Theaetetus: Certainly not, for by collecting everything into one, you've described a form that's huge and pretty complex.

Stranger: Then I suppose we know this: that the man who promises to be able to make everything by one art will be able, by the art of drawing, to produce imitations and namesakes of the things that *are*. And by displaying these drawings at a distance, he'll be able to fool the more thoughtless among the young children into believing that he's eminently capable of accomplishing in deed whatever he wanted to do.

C *Theaetetus:* Of course.

Stranger: What next: Shouldn't we expect that there's some other, speech-related art by which it happens to be possible again to enchant the young—this time with speeches through the ears—while they are yet standing off at a distance from the affairs of truth? These people display spoken images of all things so as to make it seem that they are spoken truly and hence that the speaker is the wisest of all in all things.

D *Theaetetus:* Why wouldn't there be some other such art?

Stranger: Won't most of those who were listening at the time, Theaetetus, be compelled to change the opinions they formed, once enough time has gone by for them and age advances and they are thrown in closely with things as they *are* and are forced through suffering to get a clear hold of these things? And so, won't what was

E great appear small, and what was easy hard? And won't all the speech-apparitions be overturned every which way by the deeds that have come home to them in the doings of life?

Theaetetus: As far as someone of my age can judge. But I think I too am one of those who are still standing off at a distance.

Stranger: Therefore all of us here will try—and are now trying—to bring you as close as possible without the sufferings. But tell me this about the

235 A sophist: Is it now clear that he's one of the enchanters, since he's an imitator of the things that *are*? Or are we still hesitating, in case he turns out truly to have knowledge about all those things he seems able to debate about?

Theaetetus: How could he, stranger? Surely, given what's been said, it's now fairly clear that he's one of those who take part in playing jokes.

Stranger: Then certainly we must set him down as a sort of enchanter and hence imitator.

Theaetetus: We must.

Stranger: Come, it's our job right now not to let the beast get away any
B longer. For we've almost got him surrounded, caught in a net of those
devices men use in arguments about such things. So at least he won't
escape this—

Theaetetus: What?

Stranger: The charge that he's some one of the wonder-working kind.

Theaetetus: This seems right about him to me too.

Stranger: Then it has been resolved: We are to divide the image-
making art as quickly as possible and make our descent within it.
Should the sophist confront us right off, we are to seize him by order
C of Royal Reason, and we are to display our quarry as we hand him
over. Should, however, the sophist plunge down somewhere among
the parts of the imitative art, we are to follow him closely, always
dividing the part that receives him, until he is caught. In any event,
neither he nor any other kind is ever to boast of escaping the Way of
those who can pursue matters both piecemeal and over all.

Theaetetus: You've put it well; we must do it in just this way.

Stranger: Then according to our earlier way of dividing, I for one now
D appear to see two forms of the imitative art. But as yet I don't seem able
to understand in which of the two the "look" we're seeking turns up.

Theaetetus: Still, you speak first and divide for us the pair you mean.

Stranger: I see the likeness-making art as one part within the
imitative. And this art is present above all when someone produces
the generating of an imitation according to the proportions of the
E model in length and breadth and depth and, in addition to this,
gives it colors that suit each of its parts.

Theaetetus: What? Don't all those who imitate anything try to do
this?

Stranger: Not those who sculpt or draw some large-scale work, I
suppose. For if they were to render the true proportions of beautiful things, you know that the upper parts would appear smaller than
236 A they should and the lower parts larger. The reason is that the former
are seen by us at a distance but the latter close up.

Theaetetus: By all means.

Stranger: So isn't it the case that craftsmen nowadays, bidding farewell
to the truth, produce within their images not the genuine proportions
but only those that seem beautiful?

Theaetetus: By all means.

Stranger: Then isn't it just to call the other image, since it is like, a *likeness*?

Theaetetus: Yes.

B *Stranger:* And mustn't we call the part of the imitative art that applies itself to this just what we called it before—"likeness-making?"

Theaetetus: We must.

Stranger: And what about this: What do we call that which appears to be like the beautiful only because it's seen from an unbeautiful point of view, but which, if someone were empowered to see things that large adequately, wouldn't even seem to be like what it claims to be like? Since it appears but is not like, shouldn't we call it an *apparition*?

Theaetetus: Certainly.

C *Stranger:* And isn't this a huge part both of painting and of the imitative art as a whole?

Theaetetus: Of course.

Stranger: Then wouldn't we be most correct to name the art that produces an apparition but not a likeness "apparition-making"?

Theaetetus: Very much so.

Stranger: This, then, is the dual form of image-making I meant: likeness-making and apparition-making.

Theaetetus: Correct.

Stranger: And even now I'm not yet able to behold clearly what I was of two minds about then—in which of the two the sophist must be put. D But the man is wondrous in his very being and utterly difficult to keep in our sights, since even now he's fled, in very good and clever fashion, down into a form that offers no passage for our tracking.

Theaetetus: So it seems.

Stranger: Are you assenting, then, because you recognize this to be the case? Or did some impulse sweep you along to speedy assent because the account has accustomed you to it?

Theaetetus: What do you mean? And why did you say that?

Stranger: The speculation we're in, bless you, is genuinely difficult in E every way. For this business of appearing and seeming but not being, and of saying things but not true ones—all these matters are always full of perplexity, now as in time past. For how, in speaking, one is to say or to opine that falsehoods genuinely *are*, and not, in having 237 A uttered this, be hemmed in by contradiction—this, Theaetetus, is in every way difficult to understand.

Theaetetus: Why is that?

Stranger: This sentence has dared to suppose that Non-being *is*. For otherwise falsehood would not come to be what it is. But Parmenides the Great, my boy, beginning when we were boys and to the end, would testify stoutly and speak repeatedly—in prose as well as in meter—thus

> This [he says] should not ever prevail in your thought: that the things that *are not, are*; Rather do keep your mind well shut off from just this way in searching.

B So that's the testimony from him; and the account itself, when put to a fair test, would show what he means most of all. Let's look first at this, if it doesn't make any difference to you.

Theaetetus: Do suppose that I will agree to whatever you wish; and when you see how the argument is best pursued, go that way yourself and take me down that path.

Stranger: I'll do that. And tell me: I suppose we do dare to pronounce Utter-non-being?

Theaetetus: Of course.

Stranger: If, then, not as a point of contention or a joke but in earnest,
C one of Parmenides' listeners had to think it out and to answer the question, "Where must this name Non-being be applied?," how do we think he would use the name—for what purpose and for what sort of thing? And how would he show this to the one who inquired?

Theaetetus: You asked a hard question, one that leaves someone like me, I might say, entirely at an impasse.

Stranger: But this at least is clear: that "Non-being" must not be applied to any beings.

Theaetetus: How could it be?

Stranger: Now if it could not be applied to a being, then anyone who applied it to "some" would not apply it correctly.

Theaetetus: How could he?

D *Stranger:* And this is in any case apparent to us: that we always use this expression "some" of a being. For to use it alone, naked and isolated, as it were, from all the beings—that's impossible. Or isn't it?

Theaetetus: It's impossible.

Stranger: Are you then agreeing because you see that there's a necessity for him who says "some" to be saying "some *one*"?

Theaetetus: Just so.

Stranger: For you will say that singular "some" is in fact a sign of one, dual "some" of two, and plural "some" of many.

Theaetetus: Of course.

E *Stranger:* And so it's utterly necessary, it seems, that he who says "not some" is saying no-thing at all.

Theaetetus: Utterly necessary.

Stranger: Then we mustn't grant even this much: that such a man speaks although he says nothing. Mustn't we instead declare that whoever tries to pronounce non-being does not even speak?

Theaetetus: Then the account would reach its ultimate perplexity.

238 A *Stranger:* Don't start talking big yet. For, bless you, the biggest and first of perplexities in these matters is still before us. For this perplexity turns out to be about the very beginning of the matter.

Theaetetus: What do you mean? Speak and don't hold anything back.

Stranger: I suppose that one of the things that *are* may come to be joined with another?

Theaetetus: Of course.

Stranger: But will we claim that one of the things that *are* can come to be joined to non-being?

Theaetetus: How could that be?

Stranger: Now we set down number as a whole among the things that *are*.

B *Theaetetus:* Certainly, if we must set down anything else as being.

Stranger: Then let us in no way attempt to apply plurality or unity of number to Non-being.

Theaetetus: The account asserts, it seems, that it would not be right for us to attempt this.

Stranger: How, then, could someone utter through his mouth or even grasp in his thought Non-beings or Non-being apart from number?

Theaetetus: Say where number comes in.

Stranger: Whenever we say "non-beings," aren't we attempting to
C add plurality of number to them?

Theaetetus: Certainly.

Stranger: And whenever "non-being," unity?

Theaetetus: Very clearly.

Stranger: And yet, we claim it's neither just nor correct to link being with non-being.

Theaetetus: You speak very truly.

Stranger: Do you see then, that it's not possible correctly to utter or speak or think Non-being all by itself—that it is unthinkable and unspeakable and unutterable and irrational?

Theaetetus: That's altogether so.

D *Stranger:* Then did I speak falsely just now when I said I was going to speak of the biggest perplexity concerning it?

Theaetetus: Can we speak of one still bigger than this?

Stranger: You're marvelous! Don't you see that by the very things we've said, Non-being puts its refuter too into perplexity, and that as a result, whenever someone attempts to refute it, he's compelled to contradict himself about it?

Theaetetus: What do you mean? Speak still more clearly.

Stranger: You mustn't look for greater clarity within me. For while
E supposing that Non-being must participate in neither one nor many, a little while ago and right now I've spoken of it as one. For I am saying "Non-being." You do understand?

Theaetetus: Yes.

Stranger: And yet just a little while ago, I claimed: It *is* unutterable and unspeakable and irrational. Do you follow me?

Theaetetus: Of course I follow.

Stranger: Then in trying to attach "to be," I was contradicting what
239 A was said earlier.

Theaetetus: Apparently.

Stranger: What about this: In attaching "to be," wasn't I conversing with it as though it were a one?

Theaetetus: Yes.

Stranger: And furthermore, in calling it irrational and inexpressible and unutterable, wasn't I making my speech as though to a one?

Theaetetus: Of course.

Stranger: But we are affirming that if indeed someone is to speak correctly, he must not mark it off either as one or as many or even summon it at all; for even with this very act of accosting he'd be addressing it in the form of a one.

Theaetetus: Altogether so.

B *Stranger:* In that case, alas, what more can be said on my behalf? For in time past and at present you would find me worsted in the refutation of Non-being. So as I was saying, let's not keep looking in my speech for correct speaking about Non-being. But come now, let's look for it in you.

Theaetetus: What are you saying?

Stranger: Come on now, since you are young, exert yourself well and nobly for us with all your power! Try to utter something correct about Non-being, adding to it neither being nor unity nor plurality of number.

C *Theaetetus:* But a great and absurd zeal for the undertaking would have to possess me if, seeing you suffer all these things, I were to undertake it myself.

Stranger: Well if that's the way it looks to you, let's bid farewell to you and me. But until we hit upon someone who has the power to do this, let's say that the sophist, in the sneakiest way, has slunk down into a place with no passage.

Theaetetus: It very much appears that way.

Stranger: So then, if we say that he has some apparition-making art,

D he'll easily get a hold on us for our want of words and twist our arguments into their contraries. When we call him "image-maker," he'll interrogate us about what in the world we mean by "image." So, Theaetetus, we must see how one is to answer the young man on this question.

Theaetetus: It's clear that we'll say "the images in water and in mirrors, and what's more, painted ones and sculpted ones and all the other things which, although of this sort, are different."

E *Stranger:* You show, Theaetetus, that you've never seen a sophist.

Theaetetus: Why?

Stranger: He'll seem to you to have his eyes shut or not to have any at all.

Theaetetus: How's that?

Stranger: When you give him this answer—if you speak to him of something in mirrors or of molded figurines—he'll laugh at your words when you speak to him as if he could see. And he'll pretend to recognize

240 A neither mirrors nor water surfaces nor vision in general, but he'll ask you only about what comes from your words.

Theaetetus: What's that?

Stranger: What runs through all of these that you said were many and yet thought worthy to call by one name, uttering "image" for them all as if they were one thing. So speak and defend yourself, and don't in any way give in to the man.

Theaetetus: But stranger, what would we say an image was if not another such thing made similar to the true one?

Stranger: Are you saying "another such true one," or in what sense
B are you using "such"?

Theaetetus: No way in the sense of "true," but rather "like."

Stranger: But by "the true" you mean "what genuinely *is*"?

Theaetetus: Just so.

Stranger: Well then, isn't the "not true" the contrary of the true?

Theaetetus: Certainly.

Stranger: Then you say the like genuinely *is not*, if you call it "not true."

Theaetetus: Yet in some way it *is*, after all.

Stranger: But not truly, as you say.

Theaetetus: No, I admit, except it's genuinely a likeness.

Stranger: Then what we call a likeness genuinely *is* in not *genuinely*
being.

C *Theaetetus:* Non-being does risk being entwined in some such interweaving
with Being, and a very absurd one too.

Stranger: Of course it's absurd. You see, then, that through this interchange
the many-headed sophist has once more compelled us to agree, though not
willingly, that Non-being somehow *is*.

Theaetetus: I see it all too well.

Stranger: Well then, will we be able to remain consonant with ourselves in
marking off his expertise?

Theaetetus: Where are you looking? And what are you afraid of when you
say that?

D *Stranger:* Regarding apparitions, whenever we say that he deceives
and that his expertise is a sort of "deception-inducing," then shall
we say that our soul is induced by his expertise to opine falsely? Or
what shall we say?

Theaetetus: Say that, for what else would we say?

Stranger: And in turn opinion will be false when it opines the contrary of
things that *are*?

Theaetetus: Yes, the contrary.

Stranger: Then do you say that false opinion opines things that *are not*?

Theaetetus: It's necessary.

E *Stranger:* Does it opine that things that are not, are *not*, or that things that
in no way are, *are* somehow?

Theaetetus: It must be that things that are not, *are* somehow, if anyone is ever to think falsely even in the slightest.

Stranger: Well, and does it not also opine that things that wholly *are*, in no way *are*?

Theaetetus: Yes.

Stranger: And this too is falsehood?

Theaetetus: This too.

Stranger: And a sentence will, I think, be considered false in the same way: when it says that things that *are*, are *not* and that things that are *not*, *are*.

Theaetetus: In what other way could it happen?

Stranger: In almost no other way. But the sophist won't assent to this. Or by what shift will any reasonable man grant it, when the matters we came to agreement about earlier were fully agreed to be unutterable and unspeakable and irrational and unthinkable? Do we understand, Theaetetus, what he's saying?

Theaetetus: Of course we understand: he'll claim that when we dare to say that false things are present in opinions and statements, we're contradicting what was said just now. For, he'll claim, we keep on being compelled to attach Being to Non-being, although we fully agreed just now that this is the most impossible of all things.

Stranger: You've remembered correctly. But the hour has clearly come for us to take counsel on what must be done about the sophist. For you see how many and how inventive are the objections and impasses that arise whenever we track him by putting him in the art of falsehood-workers and enchanters.

Theaetetus: Very much so.

Stranger: In fact we've gone through only a small part of them, since they are, so to speak, unlimited in number.

Theaetetus: If that's the case, it would be impossible, it seems, to get hold of the sophist.

Stranger: What? Are we such softies that we're going to give in now?

Theaetetus: I'm not saying we should, not if we can get a hold on the man even a little.

Stranger: You'll pardon me then and be content, as you've just suggested, if in some way we pull back a bit from his mighty argument?

Theaetetus: Of course I'll pardon you.

Stranger: Then I'll make one further request of you.

Theaetetus: What's that?

Stranger: Don't suppose that I'm becoming a sort of parricide.

Theaetetus: What!

Stranger: In defending ourselves we'll be compelled to put the argument of my father Parmenides to the test, and to force our way to the conclusion that Non-being in some respect *is* and that Being in turn *is not* in some way.

Theaetetus: It's apparent that we must do battle for some such thing in our arguments.

Stranger: Of course it's apparent, even to a blind man, as the saying goes. For as long as these things are neither refuted nor agreed upon, hardly anyone who talks about false speeches or opinions—whether about images or likenesses or imitations or apparitions themselves or about all the arts that concern them—hardly anyone will be able to avoid being ridiculous, since he'll be compelled to contradict himself.

Theaetetus: Very true.

242 A *Stranger:* That's exactly why we must now dare to take on the paternal argument. Or else, if some scruple prevents us from doing this, we must let the whole thing go.

Theaetetus: But nothing at all should prevent us in any way whatsoever.

Stranger: In that case, I'll make yet a third little request of you.

Theaetetus: You have only to say what it is.

Stranger: A little while ago I spoke and said that I've always shrunk back from the refutation in these matters, and so I do right now.

Theaetetus: That's what you said.

Stranger: In fact, I'm afraid that on account of what I said, this time you'll think I'm mad for having turned my position upside down on B the spur of the moment. You see, it's for your sake that we'll take on the refutation of the argument—if, that is, we do refute it.

Theaetetus: Since I won't think anything you're doing is at all discordant, should you set out on this refutation and proof, do so boldly as far as that's concerned.

Stranger: Come then, with what beginning could one begin a danger-ridden argument? Ah, my boy, I think the most compelling way for us to take is this.

Theaetetus: What way?

Stranger: First of all, to examine what now seems evident, so that C we're not in confusion about these things and easily agree with one another as if our judgement were good.

Theaetetus: Say more clearly what you mean.

Stranger: It seems to me that Parmenides and everybody else talked to us casually when they rushed into a judgement about marking off the "how many" and the "what sort" of beings.

Theaetetus: How so?

Stranger: Some sort of story, that's what each appears to me to have told us, as though we were children. One tells us that the beings are three, that at one time some of them make war on each other some-
D how, and at another time, when they've become friends, they have marriages and children and provide nurture for their offspring. An-other, who says the beings are two—"wet and dry" or "hot and cold"—settles them and gives them away in marriage. And the Eleatic tribe in our regions, starting from Xenophanes[3] and even before that, explains in stories that "all things," as they are called, are in fact *one.* Then some
E Ionian and later some Sicilian Muses realized that it was safest to weave together both views and say that Being is both many and one, and that it is held together by enmity and friendship. The reason is that it continuously comes together in differing with itself—so say the more high-strung of the Muses. But the softer ones relaxed this constant tension and say that sometimes, under the influence of
243 A Aphrodite, the All is one and friendly, and at other times it is many and at war with itself through some strife. Whether anyone of them spoke truly about these things or not, it is harsh and discordant to censure so heavily such famous and ancient men. But this much can be asserted without reproach.

Theaetetus: What's that?

Stranger: That they too often overlooked and made too little of us ordinary people. For without caring whether we follow them as they
B speak or are left behind, each of them goes on to reach his own conclusion.

Theaetetus: What do you mean?

Stranger: When anyone of them makes utterance and says that many or one or two *are* or have come to be or are becoming, and again, that hot is mixed with cold, and somewhere else hypothesizes separations and mixtures—do you, Theaetetus, ever understand what in the gods' name they are saying? For my part, when I was younger, when-ever someone would mention this thing that now perplexes us,

---

[3] Aristotle reports that Xenophanes was "a unifier—the first of them—for Parmenides was said to be one who learned from him . . ." (*Metaphysics* 986 b 22).

namely Non-being, I thought I had a precise understanding of it. But now you see how far we've gone into an impasse about it.

C *Theaetetus:* I do see.

Stranger: Perhaps, then, it may be that our souls have no less caught the same condition concerning Being: we claim to have clear passage and to understand, whenever someone utters it, but we don't claim this about the other, although we're in a similar situation with respect to both.

Theaetetus: Perhaps.

Stranger: And let's say the same thing about the other matters we spoke of before.

Theaetetus: Entirely so.

Stranger: Many of these matters we'll look into later, if you agree, but
D for now let's look into their greatest and first originator.

Theaetetus: What are you referring to? Or is it clear that you're saying we must first track down what in the world those who speak of Being think they are revealing?

Stranger: Theaetetus, you've caught on right away. For I say that at this point we must conduct our pursuit by examining them as if they were present. Here's how: "Come then, all of you who say that all
E things are hot or cold or some such two—what are you uttering that applies to both, when you declare both and each to *be*? How are we to understand this 'to be' of yours? Is it a third besides those two, and should we posit that, according to you, the All is three and no longer two? For surely when you call the one or the other of the pair Being, you're not saying that both similarly *are*. For in both cases, the pair would be pretty much one but not two."

Theaetetus: What you say is true.

Stranger: "But do you want to call both together being?"

Theaetetus: Perhaps.

244 A *Stranger:* "But friends," we'll declare, "even so, the two would be said to be very clearly one."

Theaetetus: You've spoken very correctly.

Stranger: "Then since we've reached an impasse, you make sufficiently apparent to us what in the world you want to point to whenever you utter 'being.' For it's clear that you've recognized these things for a long time, while we supposed we knew earlier, but have now reached an impasse. So teach us this very thing first of all, so that we may not opine that we understand what's said by you when the

B complete contrary is the case." In saying and demanding such things of these men and the others who say that the All is more than one, will we, my boy, strike a false note?

Theaetetus: Not in the least.

Stranger: And what about this: Mustn't we learn as best we can from those who say that the All is one what in the world they say Being is?

Theaetetus: Of course.

Stranger: Then let them answer this: "I suppose you claim that one alone *is*." "We do," they will claim. Isn't this so?

Theaetetus: Yes.

Stranger: "What about this: Do you call something 'being'?"

Theaetetus: Yes.

C *Stranger:* "Is it the very thing you call 'one'—using two names for the same thing—or what?"

Theaetetus: What's their answer to this, Stranger?

Stranger: It's clear, Theaetetus, that it's not at all easy for the man who assumes this hypothesis to answer what's now being asked—or anything else.

Theaetetus: How so?

Stranger: I suppose it's ridiculous for the man who posits nothing but one to agree that two names *are*.

Theaetetus: Of course.

Stranger: And all in all it would not be reasonable to be receptive to

D one who says that any name *is*.

Theaetetus: In what way?

Stranger: I suppose that in positing the name as other than the thing, he asserts a pair.

Theaetetus: Yes.

Stranger: Moreover, if he posits the name as the same as the thing, either he'll be compelled to say that it's the name of nothing; or if he claims that it's the name of something, it will follow that the name is only the name of a name and of nothing else.

Theaetetus: Just so.

Stranger: And "the One" will be the name that goes with One; and the One will in turn go with the name.

Theaetetus: That's necessary.

Stranger: And what about this: Will they claim that the Whole is other than the One that *is* or the same as it?

E *Theaetetus:* They surely will and do claim that it's the same.

Stranger: Well then, if the Whole is, just as Parmenides too says,

> Like to the mass of a sphere nicely rounded from every direction,
> Out from the center well-matched in all ways. For no greater
> Nor any smaller it needs must turn out, both on this and on that side,

then in being such, Being has a center and extremes, and in having these, it must with every necessity have parts. Or how is it?

Theaetetus: Just so.

245 A *Stranger:* Still, nothing prevents that which is divided into parts from being affected by the One over all its parts, and from being in this way one, since it is both all and whole.

Theaetetus: Certainly.

Stranger: But isn't it impossible for what is so affected to be itself the One itself?

Theaetetus: How's that?

Stranger: Surely, it is necessary that the truly One be declared entirely partless, according to the correct account.

Theaetetus: It must be.

B *Stranger:* But that other sort of one, since it is made out of many parts, will not harmonize with this account.

Theaetetus: I understand.

Stranger: Then is it the case that Being will be both one and whole in this way—by being affected by the One? Or shall we deny that Being is in any way whole?

Theaetetus: You've thrown a tough choice before us.

Stranger: Certainly, what you say is very true. For Being, if it is *affected* so as to be somehow one, will show itself to be not the same as the One, and all things will in fact be more than one.

Theaetetus: Yes.

Stranger: And yet, if indeed Being is not a whole through having been C affected by the One, and if the Whole itself *is*, then it turns out that Being lacks itself.

Theaetetus: Entirely so.

Stranger: And so, according to this account, Being, since it is deprived of itself, will be not-being.

Theaetetus: Just so.

Stranger: And again, all things come to be more than one, since both Being and the Whole have separately taken on a nature peculiar to each.

Theaetetus: Yes.

Stranger: But if the Whole *is not* at all, these same difficulties pertain
D to Being. And in addition to not being, it could not even have ever come to be.

Theaetetus: Why is that?

Stranger: What comes to be has always come to be as a whole. So that if someone doesn't posit the Whole among the things that *are*, he must address neither beinghood nor becoming as something that *is*.

Theaetetus: That seems to be altogether the case.

Stranger: And furthermore, it's necessary that the Non-whole not be "so much" at all. For if it is "so much," however much that might be, it is necessarily that much as a whole.

Theaetetus: Exactly.

Stranger: And so, thousands of other difficulties, each bringing on
E boundless impasses, will come to light for the one who says that Being is either two or only one.

Theaetetus: All the difficulties that are now dawning upon us make that pretty clear. For they are linked together, the one sprung from the other, bringing greater and more grievous wandering in what we kept saying earlier.

Stranger: Moreover, we haven't gone through all those who speak precisely about Being and Non-being; however, let this suffice. But we must turn our gaze to those who speak in a different way, so that we may
246 A know from every quarter that there's no easier passage when we say what Being is than what Non-being is.

Theaetetus: In that case, we must pass on to those as well.

Stranger: And it does seem that among them there is a sort of Battle of the Gods and Giants,[4] because of the dispute they have with each other about beinghood.

Theaetetus: How so?

Stranger: Those on one side drag all things down out of the heavens and the invisible realm, literally grabbing rocks and trees with their hands. They grasp all such things and maintain strenuously that that alone *is* which allows for some touching and embracing. For they
B mark off beinghood and body as the same; and if anyone from the

---

[4] The attempt of the earth-born monsters called "giants" to dethrone the Olympian gods. The giants lost.

other side says that something is that has no body, they despise him totally and don't want to listen to anything else.

Theaetetus: These certainly are terrible men you've told of. For even I have already run into packs of them.

Stranger: That's why those who dispute with them defend themselves very cautiously out of some invisible place on high, forcing true beinghood to be certain thought-things and disembodied forms. But C the bodies of their opponents and what these men call truth, they bust up into small pieces in their arguments and call it, instead of beinghood, some sort of swept-along becoming. And between these two, Theaetetus, a tremendous sort of battle over these things has forever been joined.

Theaetetus: True.

Stranger: Let us therefore obtain an account from both kinds of men in turn on behalf of the beinghood they posit.

Theaetetus: How then shall we obtain it?

Stranger: From those who posit beinghood in the forms it's easier. For they are more tame. But from those who drag everything by force into D body it's harder, and perhaps even close to impossible. But this is how it seems to me we have to deal with them.

Theaetetus: How?

Stranger: The chief thing would be, if it were in any way possible, to make them better in deed. But if there's no room for that, let's make them better in speech. Let's assume they'd answer in a more law-abiding way than they're now willing to do. For what's been agreed on by better people has more authority than what's agreed on by worse. But we don't care about these people—it's the truth we seek.

E *Theaetetus:* Absolutely right.

Stranger: Then urge these people who've become better to answer you, and interpret what's said by them.

Theaetetus: I will.

Stranger: Let them say whether they claim there is such a thing as a mortal animal.

Theaetetus: Of course.

Stranger: And don't they agree that this is an ensouled body?

Theaetetus: Entirely so.

Stranger: Positing soul as one of the things that *are*?

247 A *Theaetetus:* Yes.

Stranger: What about this: Don't they affirm that one soul is just and another unjust, and that one is thoughtful and another thoughtless?

Theaetetus: Certainly.

Stranger: But don't they affirm that each soul becomes just by the possession and presence of justice, and becomes the contrary by the possession and presence of their contraries?

Theaetetus: Yes, they also affirm these things.

Stranger: Yet surely they'll affirm that what has the power to become present to or absent from something certainly *is* something.

Theaetetus: They certainly do affirm this.

B *Stranger:* Then since justice and thoughtfulness and the rest of virtue and their contraries *are*, and since, moreover, the soul within which these arise *is*, do they affirm that any of them is visible and touchable or that all are invisible?

Theaetetus: That hardly any of these at least is visible.

Stranger: And what about the things we mentioned? Do they assert that *they* have some body?

Theaetetus: They no longer respond to all this in the same way. But the soul itself seems to them to possess a sort of body; and as for thoughtfulness and each of the other things you were asking about—
C they're ashamed at daring either to agree that they are not among the things that *are* or to maintain strenuously that all these things are bodies.

Stranger: Clearly, Theaetetus, our men have become better, since the earth-sown and earth-born[5] among them would feel shame at none of this. Instead they'd contend that whatever they have no power to squeeze in their hands is—all of it—for just this reason nothing at all.

Theaetetus: You're saying pretty much what they think.

Stranger: Then let's go back to questioning them. For if they're willing to grant that any of the things that *are*, however small, is bodiless, that's
D enough. Then they must tell us what is the inborn nature common to both these things and those that have body, that is, what they have in view when they assert that both *are*. But perhaps they'd be perplexed. If they have been affected in this way, consider whether—if we made them an offer—they'd be willing to accept and agree that Being is this sort of thing.

Theaetetus: What sort? Speak up, and we'll soon know.

---

[5] Cadmus, the mythical founder of Thebes, killed a dragon whose teeth he sowed in the earth to reap a harvest of mutually murderous aboriginal warriors, "the Sown;" the survivors became the nobility of the city.

Stranger: I say, then, that what possesses any sort of power—whether for making anything at all, of whatever nature, other than it is or for
E being affected even the least bit by the meagerest thing, even if only once—I say that all this *is* in its very being. For I set down as a boundary marking off the things that *are*, that their being is nothing else but *power*.

Theaetetus: Well, seeing that they themselves have nothing better than this to say at present, they accept it.

Stranger: Beautiful. Perhaps later some other boundary may become
248 A apparent to us and to them. For now let this stand as something agreed upon by us and those men.

Theaetetus: It stands.

Stranger: Then let's approach the others, the Friends of the Forms. And you interpret for us what's said on their side too.

Theaetetus: I will.

Stranger: "You speak of becoming and divide off beinghood as something separate from it, I suppose. Don't you?"

Theaetetus: Yes.

Stranger: "And you declare that with the body, through sensing, we commune with becoming, while with the soul, through reasoning, we relate to genuine beinghood, which always persists in just the same condition, while becoming is in a different condition at different times."

B *Theaetetus:* That's certainly what we declare.

Stranger: "But, you best of all men, what shall we declare you mean by this 'communing' that spans both?" Isn't it the very thing we said just now?

Theaetetus: What was that?

Stranger: A being affected or a doing arising from some power and whose source is the coming together of things, one against the other. Maybe, Theaetetus, you don't hear their answer to this; but I do, perhaps because of my habitual dealings with them.

Theaetetus: Then what account do they give when they speak?

C *Stranger:* They don't grant us the very thing we said just now to the earth-born about beinghood.

Theaetetus: What was that?

Stranger: I suppose we set down the following boundary for the things that are as adequate: "whenever the power to be affected or to act is present in something even in the slightest"?

56

Theaetetus: Yes.

Stranger: In response to this, they say that becoming partakes of a power of being affected and doing; but they declare that the power of neither of these fits with beinghood.

Theaetetus: And isn't there something in what they say?

Stranger: Yes, to which we must say that we still need to learn from
D them more clearly whether they agree that the soul recognizes and that beinghood is recognized.

Theaetetus: Surely they declare this much.

Stranger: What about this: "Do you declare that recognizing or being recognized is a doing, or a being affected, or both? Or that one is a being affected and the other a doing? Or that neither has a share in either of these in any way whatsoever?"

Theaetetus: Clearly that neither has a share in either, or else they'd be contradicting what they said earlier.

Stranger: I understand. This at least is the case: that if in fact to
E recognize is to do something, then it follows in turn that the thing recognized necessarily is affected. Now beinghood, according to this account, is recognized by the act of recognition; and insofar as it is recognized, it is to that extent *moved* through being affected, which, we declare, would not have come about for what keeps still.

Theaetetus: Right.

249 A *Stranger:* What the Zeus! Shall we be that easily persuaded that motion and life and soul and thought are truly not present in utterly complete Being? That it neither lives nor thinks; but awful and holy, not possessed of mind, it stands there, not to be moved?

Theaetetus: That, Stranger, would be a terrible account to grant.

Stranger: But are we to say that it has mind and not life?

Theaetetus: How could we?

Stranger: But do we say that both of these are in it, and then go on to deny that it has them in a soul?

Theaetetus: And in what other way would it have them?

Stranger: Then will we really say that it has mind and life and soul and yet, although ensouled, stands entirely immovable?

B *Theaetetus:* To me that appears entirely irrational.

Stranger: So we must grant that the moved and motion are things that *are*.

Theaetetus: Of course.

Stranger: Thus the outcome is, Theaetetus, that if the things that *are* are immovable, there is mind in nothing about nothing nowhere.

Theaetetus: Exactly.

Stranger: And yet, if we grant that all things are borne about and moving, we shall exclude, by that very account, this same mind from the things that *are*.

Theaetetus: How?

Stranger: Do you think that being in the same respect and in like
C manner and about the same thing would ever come to be apart from rest?

Theaetetus: Never.

Stranger: Well then, without these do you see how mind could *be* or ever come to be anywhere?

Theaetetus: Not in the least.

Stranger: So we must surely fight, using every argument, against him who first makes knowledge or thoughtfulness or mind disappear and then makes strong assertions about anything in any way.

Theaetetus: Definitely.

Stranger: Then for the man who is philosophical and thus most respects these things, there is every compulsion, it seems, just because of them, not to be receptive to people who say that the All is at rest either as a one or even in many forms. Nor again must he listen at all to
D those who move Being every which way. But he must assert—as in the children's prayer "Whatever is immovable and moved"—that Being and the All consist of both together.

Theaetetus: Very true.

Stranger: Well then, don't we appear at this point to have pretty well encompassed Being in an account?

Theaetetus: By all means.

Stranger: Hold it, Theaetetus! It seems to me, we're now on the verge of recognizing the perplexity that belongs to the inquiry into Being.

E *Theaetetus:* Now what! Why are you saying that?

Stranger: Don't you notice, bless you, that we're now in the fullest ignorance about it, just when we appear to ourselves to be saying something?

Theaetetus: It does seem so to me. But how we slipped into that condition I don't understand at all.

Stranger: Then look more closely to see if in agreeing to these things

now, we might not justly be asked exactly what we ourselves earlier
250 A on were asking those who say that the All is hot and cold.

Theaetetus: What do you mean? Remind me.

Stranger: By all means. And I'll try to do it by questioning you just
as we questioned those men then, in order that we may both make
some progress.

Theaetetus: That's right.

Stranger: Well then: Don't you say that Rest and Motion are most
contrary to one another?

Theaetetus: Of course.

Stranger: And yet you claim this at least: that both and each of
them alike *are*.

B *Theaetetus:* I certainly do claim this.

Stranger: Is it the case, whenever you grant that they *are*, that you
mean that both and each of them are in motion?

Theaetetus: In no way.

Stranger: But do you mean to indicate that both of them are at rest
when you say they both *are*?

Theaetetus: How could I?

Stranger: Then do you posit Being as some third thing in the soul
beyond these, as if Rest and Motion were embraced by it? And is it
through taking them together and focusing on the community of
their beinghood that you say that both of them *are*?

C *Theaetetus:* We truly do seem to divine that Being is some third
thing, whenever we say that Rest and Motion *are*.

Stranger: Therefore Being is not Motion and Rest both together
but something other than these.

Theaetetus: It seems so.

Stranger: Then according to its own nature, Being is neither at rest
nor in motion.

Theaetetus: That's about right.

Stranger: Where, then, can the man who wants to establish something
clear about it for himself still turn his thought?

Theaetetus: Where indeed!

D *Stranger:* I certainly suppose there's nowhere he can still turn easily. For if something isn't in motion, how is it not at rest? Or again,
how is that which is in no way at rest not in motion? Yet Being has
now come to light for us outside both of these. Is that possible?

Theaetetus: It's the most impossible thing of all.

Stranger: Well then, we'd do right to remember the following in addition to these matters.

Theaetetus: What?

Stranger: That when we were asked to what in the world one must apply the name of Non-being, we were hemmed in by total perplexity. Do you remember?

Theaetetus: Of course.

E *Stranger:* We're not in any less perplexity now about Being, are we?

Theaetetus: To me, Stranger, if I may say so, we appear to be in greater perplexity.

Stranger: Well then, let this matter be set down here as utterly perplexing. And since Being and Non-being have both had an equal share in perplexity, there's now hope that in whatever way one of them comes to light more dimly or more clearly, so the other will come to light.

251 A And again, if we're able to see neither of them, we'll at least push our account through both at once as fittingly as we can.

Theaetetus: Beautiful.

Stranger: Then let's say according to what habit we keep calling this same thing by many names.

Theaetetus: What do you mean? Give an example.

Stranger: Well, we speak of man, I suppose, but give him many titles: we add colors to him and shapes and sizes and vices and virtues. In all

B these attributions and thousands of others, we declare him to be not only man but also good and infinitely many other things. And the same account holds for other things as well: we assume that each thing is one but take it back by speaking of it as many and with many names.

Theaetetus: True.

Stranger: Which is exactly why, I imagine, we've furnished a feast for youths and for oldsters late in learning. For it's handy enough for anyone to get a direct grip on the fact that it's impossible both for the many to be one and for the one to be many. And no doubt, I suppose,

C these people delight in not letting anyone say that man is good but only that good is good and man is man. As I imagine, Theaetetus, you often chance upon people that seriously pursue such things, sometimes elderly men, who are struck with wonder at such things owing to the poverty of their store of good sense and who go so far as to imagine they've discovered something superwise in this.

Theaetetus: By all means.

Stranger: Therefore, in order that our account be directed towards
all those who have ever discoursed in any way about beinghood, let's
D   address the speeches we're now about to give to these people and to
the others, with whom we've conversed before, as though we were
engaged in questioning.

Theaetetus: So what sort of things shall we ask?

Stranger: "In our own accounts, are we to attach neither beinghood
to Motion and Rest nor anything at all to anything else whatsoever but
posit things as unmixed and incapable of having a share in each other?
Or are we to bring them all together into the same place, treating them
as though they were capable of communing with each other? Or are
E   some capable and others not?" Which of these, Theaetetus, should we
say that these people choose?

Theaetetus: I'm not at all able to answer for them on these matters.

Stranger: Then why didn't you look into their consequences one at
a time and answer the questions one by one?

Theaetetus: Beautiful suggestion.

Stranger: And if you wish, let's suppose they say first of all that nothing has any power whatever for community with anything at all in any
way. Then both Motion and Rest will in no way at all participate in
beinghood?

252 A *Theaetetus:* Certainly not.

Stranger: Well then, will either one of them *be* if it doesn't commune
with beinghood?

Theaetetus: It won't.

Stranger: By this very agreement, it seems, all things have suddenly
been upset at once: the claim of those who set the All in motion,
and of those who bring it to rest as one—and all those who say that
beings are sorted by forms that are forever in just the same condition. For all these people attach the verb "to be," some saying that
all things in their very being are in motion, and others that all things
in their very being are at rest.

Theaetetus: Exactly.

B *Stranger:* And further, all those people who sometimes combine all
things and sometimes divide them, whether they divide and combine
into one and out of one limitless elements or elements that keep to a
limit—it's just the same whether they posit this as coming about by
turns or continuously: they'd be saying nothing with all these claims
if there's no intermixing at all.

Theaetetus: Right.

Stranger: Moreover, those very people who don't let us address anything at all as an other thing by reason of its community with an other's condition would be the ones who of all people pursued the argument in the most ridiculous way.

C   *Theaetetus:* How so?

Stranger: They're compelled, I suppose, to use "to be" and "apart" and "from the others" and "by itself" and thousands of other expressions about all things. Since they're powerless to keep these out of and not to bring them into their speeches, they don't need others to refute them. But, as the saying goes, they have their enemy and future opponent right at home, and as they make their way, they always carry around something uttering speech from deep inside, like that absurd ventriloquist Euricles.

D   *Theaetetus:* What you say is exactly like them as well as true.

Stranger: Well then, should we allow all things to have the power for community with one another?

Theaetetus: Even I can break that down.

Stranger: How?

Theaetetus: Because Motion itself would be altogether at rest, and Rest in turn would itself be in motion, if the two of them were to follow upon each other.

Stranger: But this, I suppose, is by the greatest necessities impossible— that Motion should be at rest, and Rest should be in motion.

Theaetetus: Of course.

Stranger: Then only the third is left.

Theaetetus: Yes.

E   *Stranger:* And surely some one of these is necessarily the case: either all things intermix, or nothing does, or some things are amenable to intermixing and some not.

Theaetetus: Of course.

Stranger: And surely the first two were found to be impossible.

Theaetetus: Yes.

Stranger: So everyone who wants to answer rightly will posit the remaining of the three.

Theaetetus: Exactly.

Stranger: Now since some things are amenable to doing this and
253   A   others not, they'd be a lot like letters. For I take it that in the case of

letters too, some don't fit with one another and others do.

Theaetetus: Of course.

Stranger: And the vowels differ from the others in passing through them all as a sort of bond, so that without some one of them it's impossible for the others to fit, one with another.

Theaetetus: Very much so.

Stranger: Then does everyone know which letters can commune with which, or does the man who means to join them need an art?

Theaetetus: He needs an art.

Stranger: Which one?

Theaetetus: The "spelling" art.

Stranger: Well then, isn't it the same with high and low sounds? The
B man who has the art of recognizing those sounds that do and do not blend is musical, while the man who doesn't comprehend is unmusical?

Theaetetus: Just so.

Stranger: And in all the other arts and non-arts, we'll find other things like these.

Theaetetus: Of course.

Stranger: Well then, since we've agreed that the kinds too are in the same condition regarding their mixing with one another, isn't it necessary for the man who intends to show rightly which of them harmonize with which and which do not receive one another, to make his way through accounts with some sort of knowledge? Isn't
C this especially so if he intends to show whether there are some kinds which, present throughout, hold the other kinds together, so that they can intermix, and again whether there are other kinds which, where there are divisions, are causes of division throughout the whole?

Theaetetus: Of course he needs knowledge, and perhaps very nearly the greatest.

Stranger: Then what in turn shall we call this knowledge, Theaetetus? Or by Zeus, have we stumbled without noticing it on the knowledge that belongs to free men? And have we, while seeking the sophist, by some chance found the philosopher first?

Theaetetus: What do you mean?

D *Stranger:* Won't we claim that it belongs to dialectical knowledge to divide according to kinds and not to regard the same form as other nor the other as the same?

Theaetetus: Yes, we'll claim this.

Stranger: Then the man who can do this has an adequate perception of one "look" extended everywhere through many things, each one of which lies apart, and also many "looks" which are other than one another and are embraced by one external to them; again, he perceives one unified E "look" composed of many wholes as well as many "looks" marked off as entirely apart. But to know this is to know how to discern, according to kind, where each is able to commune and where not.

Theaetetus: That's altogether so.

Stranger: But certainly, I imagine, you won't give the dialectical power to anyone else but the man who philosophizes purely and justly.

Theaetetus: How could one give it to anyone else?

Stranger: Then surely we'll find the philosopher in some such place both now and hereafter, if ever we search for him. This man too is 254 A difficult to see clearly; yet there's a different twist to the difficulty with the sophist and the difficulty with the philosopher.

Theaetetus: How so?

Stranger: The one runs away into the darkness of Non-being, feeling his way around it by mere practice, and is difficult to make out because of the dark of the place. Right?

Theaetetus: So it would seem.

Stranger: But the other, who is really a philosopher or lover of wisdom, always devotes himself through account-giving to the "look" of Being, and in his turn is not at all easy to see because of B the brightness of his region. For the eyes of the soul of the many are powerless to endure looking away toward the divine.

Theaetetus: That's no less likely than what you said before.

Stranger: Then soon enough we'll inquire more clearly into him, if we still want to. But as for the sophist, it's plain, I suppose, that we mustn't give up until we get an adequate view of him.

Theaetetus: Beautifully said.

Stranger: Since, therefore, it was agreed by us that some kinds are amenable to communing with one another and others not, and that some will do so with a few while others with many, and that nothing C prevents some that even run through them all from having communed with all of them—since all this has been agreed to by us, let's pull the account along with us in the following way. Let's look, not into all the forms—so that we don't get confused among many—but only into some, having selected those spoken of as greatest. Let's first look into what sort of things they are individually, then into what holds for their power for community with one another. The result will be that if we don't have the power to take hold of both Being and Non-being with complete clarity, we'll at least not come out lacking an account for them, as far as our present way of looking allows. Let's see whether it's

D in some way permissible for us to say the following and come off unpunished: that Non-being *is*, even though in its very being it *is not*.

Theaetetus: Then that's what we should do.

Stranger: Surely the greatest of the kinds are those we were going through just now: Being itself and Rest and Motion.

Theaetetus: By far the greatest.

Stranger: Moreover, we affirm that the members of one pair of them are unmixable with one another.

Theaetetus: Definitely.

Stranger: But Being is mixable with both, for I suppose both *are*.

Theaetetus: Of course.

Stranger: Then these come to be three.

Theaetetus: Certainly.

Stranger: Then each of them is other than the remaining pair but itself the same as itself.

E *Theaetetus:* Just so.

Stranger: But how in the world have we just used these terms "same" and "other"? Are they themselves a certain pair of kinds other than the first three yet always necessarily intermixed with them; and are we to look into five and not three as being the kinds that *are*? Or are

255 A we unwittingly addressing one of those three when we say "same" and "other"?

Theaetetus: Perhaps.

Stranger: But certainly Motion and Rest are neither other nor the same.

Theaetetus: How so?

Stranger: Whatever we call Motion and Rest in common—that can't be either of them.

Theaetetus: Why?

Stranger: Motion will be at rest, and Rest in turn will be in motion. With respect to both, whichever member of the pair becomes the other will compel the other to flip into the contrary of its own nature,

B since it will participate in the contrary.

Theaetetus: Exactly.

Stranger: And yet both participate in the Same and the Other.

Theaetetus: Yes.

Stranger: Then let's not say that Motion at least is either the Same or the Other, nor in its turn is Rest.

Theaetetus: Let's not.

Stranger: But then are we to think of "Being" and "Same" as in some way one?

Theaetetus: Perhaps.

C *Stranger:* But if "Being" and "Same," as a pair, signify nothing different, then when we turn back to Motion and Rest and say that both *are*, by the same token we shall be calling both the same, since they both *are*.

Theaetetus: But that's certainly impossible.

Stranger: Then it's impossible for the Same and Being to be one.

Theaetetus: Pretty much.

Stranger: So shall we posit the Same as a fourth in addition to the three forms?

Theaetetus: By all means.

Stranger: Well then, must we say that the Other is a fifth? Or is it necessary to think of "Other" and "Being" as two distinct names for one kind?

Theaetetus: Maybe.

Stranger: But I imagine you grant that of the things that *are*, some are always said to be themselves by themselves, while others are always in relation to others.

Theaetetus: Certainly.

D *Stranger:* And what is other is always in relation to an other, isn't it?

Theaetetus: Just so.

Stranger: This wouldn't be the case if Being and the Other, as a pair, were not entirely different. But if the Other partook of both the forms you granted, as does Being, there would sometimes also be an other among the others that is unrelated to any other. And yet it has now inescapably fallen out for us that whatever is other is what it is necessarily through an other.

Theaetetus: You're saying it just the way it is.

Stranger: Then the nature of the Other must be said to be a fifth
E among the forms we're selecting.

Theaetetus: Yes.

Stranger: And we shall assert that this nature has indeed run through all of them; for each one is other than the others not because of its own nature but because it participates in the look of the Other.

Theaetetus: Exactly so.

Stranger: So let's pronounce on the five in this way, taking them up one by one.

Theaetetus: How?

Stranger: First Motion—that it is altogether other than Rest. Or how should we say it?

Theaetetus: Just so.

Stranger: Then it is not Rest.

Theaetetus: In no way.

256 A *Stranger:* But it *is*, at any rate, because it participates in Being.

Theaetetus: It *is*.

Stranger: Now again, Motion is other than the Same.

Theaetetus: That's about it.

Stranger: Then it is not the Same.

Theaetetus: No indeed.

Stranger: But surely it was the same, since all things in turn participate in the Same.

Theaetetus: Very much so.

Stranger: Then we must agree and also not find it distressing that Motion is the same and is not the Same. For it's not the case, when we say it's the same and not the Same, that we've used the term similarly.

B Rather, whenever we say Motion is the same, we speak of it that way because of its participation in the Same with respect to itself. And whenever we say it is not the Same, this is in turn because of its community with the Other, because of which community, Motion is separated off from the Same and has become not it but other. So that again it is correctly said to be *not* the Same.

Theaetetus: By all means.

Stranger: Then even if Motion itself were in some way to have a share in Rest, it would not be absurd to call it "resting"?

Theaetetus: That's very right, if indeed we're going to grant that some of the kinds are amenable to mixing with one another while others are not.

C *Stranger:* And surely we achieved the demonstration of this point before our present inquiry, by proving that it's this way according to nature.

Theaetetus: Of course.

Stranger: Then let's say it again: Motion is other than the Other, just as it was different from both the Same and Rest?

Theaetetus: That's necessary.

Stranger: Then according to our present account, it is in some way *not* other as well as other.

Theaetetus: True.

Stranger: Then what about the next thing: Since we've agreed that there are five kinds we've proposed to look at and look among, shall

D we claim that Motion is other than the three yet deny that it is other than the fourth?

Theaetetus: How could we? For it's impossible to grant that their number is less than what's now come to light.

Stranger: Shall we therefore say and contend fearlessly that Motion is other than Being?

Theaetetus: Most fearlessly.

Stranger: Then isn't it clearly the case that Motion in its very being is not-being—and also being, since it partakes of Being?

Theaetetus: It's as clear as can be.

Stranger: Therefore it's necessarily the case that Non-being *is*, both in the case of Motion and with respect to all the kinds. For with respect to

E all, the nature of the Other, by producing each as other than Being, makes each not-being. So in this sense we will correctly say that all things are for the same reasons not-being and again, because they partake of Being, that they both *are* and are being.

Theaetetus: I'm afraid so.

Stranger: Then regarding each of the forms, Being is many, while Non-being is unlimited in multitude.

Theaetetus: So it seems.

257 A *Stranger:* Then we must also say that Being itself is other than the others.

Theaetetus: Necessarily.

Stranger: And also that however many the others are, in relation to so many, Being is *not*. For insofar as it is not those others, it is itself one; and again it is *not* in relation to those others, which are unlimited in number.

Theaetetus: That's pretty much the case.

Stranger: Then we must not be distressed at this either, since it is the nature of the kinds to have community with one another. But if someone doesn't grant this, let him prevail over our consequences only after he's prevailed over our earlier arguments.

Theaetetus: Very justly spoken.

B *Stranger:* Then let's look at this as well.

Theaetetus: What?

Stranger: Whenever we say Non-being, as it seems, we don't say something contrary to Being but only other.

Theaetetus: How so?

Stranger: For instance, whenever we say that something is "non-great," do we appear to you at that moment to mean by this phrase the small any more than the equal?

Theaetetus: How could we?

Stranger: Then whenever the negative is said to signify a contrary, we won't grant it, but only this: that "non" and "not," when placed
C before the names that come after them, proclaim something other than those names, or rather proclaim something other than the things to which the names uttered after the negative are given.

Theaetetus: That's altogether so.

Stranger: But let's think about this next point to see if it too seems agreeable to you.

Theaetetus: What is it?

Stranger: It appears to me that the nature of the Other is all chopped up—just like knowledge.

Theaetetus: How so?

Stranger: Knowledge also is one, I suppose; but each marked-off part
D of it that applies to some subject matter has a certain title peculiar to it. For this reason there are many so-called arts and sciences.

Theaetetus: By all means.

Stranger: Then the parts of the nature of the Other are also in this same condition, even though this nature is one.

Theaetetus: Maybe so; but let's say exactly how.

Stranger: Is there some part of the Other that is opposed to the Beautiful?

Theaetetus: There is.

Stranger: Shall we say that this is nameless or that it has some title?

Theaetetus: That it has one. For what in each case we call "non-beautiful" is the other of the nature of the Beautiful and of nothing else.

Stranger: Come then, and tell me this.

E *Theaetetus:* What?

Stranger: Has the Non-beautiful turned out to be just this—a certain other that is marked off from one certain kind among the things that *are* and again is opposed to a certain one of the things that *are*?

Theaetetus: Just so.

Stranger: Then, as it seems, the Non-beautiful turns out to be a certain opposition of being against being.

Theaetetus: Quite right.

Stranger: What then: According to this account, is the Beautiful for us any more one of the things that *are* and the Non-beautiful any less?

Theaetetus: Not at all.

258 A *Stranger:* Then the Non-great as well as the Great itself must likewise be said to *be*.

Theaetetus: Likewise.

Stranger: And in the same way, then, mustn't the Non-just be posited with the Just, in that the one *is* in no way more than its other?

Theaetetus: Certainly.

Stranger: And we shall speak of the others in the same way, since the nature of the Other has shown itself to be among the things that *are*. And if that nature *is*, it is also necessary to posit that its parts in no less degree *are*.

Theaetetus: Of course.

B *Stranger:* Then, it seems, the opposition between the nature of a part of the Other and the nature of Being (in that they are set against each other) has beinghood to no less degree—if there is sanction for saying so—than Being itself. For it signifies not the contrary of Being but only this much: its other.

Theaetetus: That's very clear.

Stranger: What then should we call this nature?

Theaetetus: Clearly Non-being, the very thing we were seeking because of the sophist.

Stranger: Is it the case then, as you were saying, that it falls short of none of the others in beinghood? And from now on must we assert

boldly that Non-being has a firm grip on its own nature? And that just
C as the Great *was* great and the Beautiful *was* beautiful, and the Non-great non-great and the Non-beautiful non-beautiful, so too and in the same way, Non-being *was* and *is* non-being, to be counted as one form among the many things that *are*? Or do we, Theaetetus, still harbor any distrust about this matter?

Theaetetus: None at all.

Stranger: Do you see then that we have disobeyed Parmenides far beyond his prohibition?

Theaetetus: What do you mean?

Stranger: I mean that we've kept pressing onward in our inquiry and have shown him more than he told us not to look into.

Theaetetus: How?

D *Stranger:* Because he says somewhere:

> This should not ever prevail in your thought: that the things that
> *are not, are*; Rather do you keep your mind well shut off from just
> this way of searching.

Theaetetus: That's what he says.

Stranger: And we've not only shown that the things that *are not, are*, but we've also declared what the form of Non-being happens to be. For we showed that the nature of the Other *is* and that it's chopped up
E and distributed through all the things that *are* in their relation to one another, and we dared to say about each part of this nature, in its opposition to Being, that this very part is in its very being Non-being.

Theaetetus: And, stranger, we seem to have told the entire and perfect truth.

Stranger: Then let no one tell us that we are declaring Non-being to be the contrary of Being and then are daring to say that this contrary *is*. For way back we bade farewell to speaking of some
259 A contrary to Being, whether it *is* or *is not*, whether it is speakable or altogether unspeakable. But as for what we've just said Non-being is, let someone either persuade us that we haven't spoken well by refuting us or—so long as he can't—he too must say just what we do: The kinds intermix with one another; and because Being and the Other have passed through all and one another, the Other, since it has participated in Being, *is* on account of this participation, yet is not that in which it has participated, but other; and since it is other, it must very clearly be non-being. On the other
B hand, Being, since it has had a share in the Other, would be other than the other kinds; and since it is other than all those, it is not

each of them nor all of them taken together, but itself. As a result, Being in turn indisputably *is not* in thousands upon thousands of cases; and the others too, taken one by one and all together, in many cases *are* and in many *are not.*

Theaetetus: True.

Stranger: And if anyone has doubts about these contrarieties, he must do his own looking and say something better than what's been said now. Or if he delights in dragging arguments about, now in C one direction and now in others, as if he'd thought up something difficult, then he's been serious about things unworthy of much seriousness—so says our current account. For this business is neither one bit clever nor difficult to discover, while the alternative, now, is at once difficult and beautiful.

Theaetetus: Which alternative?

Stranger: The one we talked about earlier, according to which, having allowed these contrarieties as possible, we're able to follow up what people say by engaging in detailed refutation whenever anyone claims that what's other is in some way the same and what's the D same is other, and to do so in the way and in the sense in which he claims either of them has been affected. But to show that the same thing is somehow other and the other the same and the big small and the similar dissimilar, and to delight in thus always bringing forward contraries in arguments—this is no true refutation and is the manifest late-born brainchild of somebody who's just gotten in touch with the things that *are.*

Theaetetus: Exactly.

Stranger: For, my good fellow, to attempt to separate off everything from everything is in other respects discordant, and what's more, E belongs to a man who is altogether unmusical and unphilosophical.

Theaetetus: Why?

Stranger: To detach each from all is the final and utter eclipse of all speech. For speech has arisen for us through the interweaving of the forms.

Theaetetus: True.

260 A *Stranger:* Observe, then, that we were in the nick of time just now in fighting it out with such people and compelling them to let one thing mix with another.

Theaetetus: To what end?

Stranger: So that for us speech would be some one of the kinds that *are.* For if we were deprived of this, we'd be deprived of philosophy—that would be the greatest thing. And furthermore, we must at the present moment reach a thorough agreement about speech—what in the world it is. But if we had it taken away from us through its being altogether nothing, I suppose we wouldn't be able to speak anymore. And we would have had it taken away from us, if we had granted that

B there was no mixing whatsoever for anything with anything else.

Theaetetus: That's certainly right. But I don't understand why we must reach some thorough agreement about speech right now.

Stranger: Maybe you'd understand most easily by following it out like this.

Theaetetus: How?

Stranger: Certainly Non-being came to light for us as some one kind that *is* and is among the others, dispersed throughout all the things that *are.*

Theaetetus: Just so.

Stranger: Then the next thing we must look into is whether it mixes with both opinion and speech.

Theaetetus: Why's that?

Stranger: If it doesn't mix with these, then it's necessary that all things

C are true; but if it does mix, then both false opinion and speech come about. For to opine or to speak things that *are not*—this, I suppose, is the false, insofar as it comes about in both thought and speech.

Theaetetus: Just so.

Stranger: But if in fact the false *is,* then there is deception.

Theaetetus: Yes.

Stranger: And surely if there is deception, then henceforth it's necessary that all things be full of both images and likenesses and also of appearance.

Theaetetus: Of course.

Stranger: But we said that the sophist had fled down into this place

D somewhere and had gone so far as to deny utterly that the false in any way *is:* "For let no one either think or speak Non-being, since in no way at all does Non-being partake of beinghood."

Theaetetus: That's how it was.

Stranger: But now, in point of fact, Non-being has come to light as partaking of Being, so that perhaps he would no longer keep up the fight along these lines; but he'd probably say that some of the forms partake of Non-being while others do not, and that speech and opinion are among

the non-partaking ones. So he'd come back fighting and claim that
E the image-making and apparition-making art—where we say he is—
in no way *is*, since opinion and speech don't commune with Non-
being. For the false, he'd claim, *is not* at all, if this community is not
established. Then for this reason we must first investigate speech and
opinion and appearance—whatever they are—so that when they have
appeared, we may observe their community with Non-being as well.
261 A And having observed that, we may show that the false *is*. And when
we have shown that, we may imprison the sophist in it, if he's liable,
or turn him loose and search for him within another kind.

Theaetetus: What was said about the sophist at the beginning,
stranger, seems to be exactly true—that his kind would be hard to
hunt down. He appears to abound in defensive problems; and when
he throws out one of these defenses, it becomes necessary first to
fight one's way through it before reaching the man himself. For now
we have scarcely breached the limits of his defense "Non-being—that
B it *is not*," and he's thrown out another one, so that we must show of
the false that it *is* in relation to both speech and opinion. And after
that there will perhaps be another, and yet another after that. And no
limit, it seems, will ever appear.

Stranger: Anyone, Theaetetus, who is able to continue advancing to
the front even a little should take heart. For what would the man who
became dispirited under these conditions do in others, where he either
made no headway or was even pushed back to the rear? "Scarcely," as
C the proverb says, "could such a one ever take a city." But now, my good
friend, since the defense of which you speak has been breached, surely
the greatest wall would have been taken by us, and the others will from
now on be easier and smaller.

Theaetetus: Beautifully said.

Stranger: First, then, let's take up speech and opinion, as I said just
now, so that we may give a more distinct account of whether Non-
being touches them, or both of these are entirely true and neither
of them is ever false.

Theaetetus: Right.

D *Stranger:* Come then, just as we were saying about the forms and
letters, let's go back and look into names in the same way. For that's
roughly where the object of our present search is appearing.

Theaetetus: What is it about names that we must pay attention to?

Stranger: Whether all fit together with one another, or none do, or
whether some are amenable and some not.

Theaetetus: Clearly the last.

Stranger: Perhaps you're saying something like this: that words said
E in a row and indicating something fit together, while those that
signify nothing in their sequence are non-fitting.

Theaetetus: What do you mean by that?

Stranger: What I supposed you assumed when you agreed with me.
For we have, it seems, a dual kind of vocal indication concerned
with beinghood.

Theaetetus: How's that?

262 A *Stranger:* It's called in one case nouns, in the other, verbs.

Theaetetus: Say what each is.

Stranger: The indication that is for actions is, we say, a verb.

Theaetetus: Yes.

Stranger: But the vocal sign applied to those themselves who do
the actions is a noun.[6]

Theaetetus: Exactly.

Stranger: Then speech is never composed of nouns alone spoken in
sequence, nor again of verbs that have been spoken apart from nouns.

Theaetetus: I don't understand this.

B *Stranger:* It's clear that you had your eye on something else when
you agreed just now. For I meant to say just this: that these words
spoken in sequence in the following way are not speech.

Theaetetus: In what way?

Stranger: For instance, "walks," "runs," "sleeps" and the rest of
the verbs that signify actions, even if someone were to say them all
in a row, do not, for all that, produce speech.

Theaetetus: Of course not.

Stranger: And again, whenever "lion," "deer," "horse" are said,
when in turn all the names of those who act out actions are named,
C according to this sequence as well no speech is yet composed. For in
neither this way nor the way mentioned before does what is uttered
indicate the action or inaction or beinghood of a thing that *is* or a
thing that *is not*, until someone blends verbs with nouns. Then they
fit together, and their first interweaving straight off becomes speech—
very nearly the first and smallest of speeches.

Theaetetus: How do you mean this?

Stranger: Whenever someone says "man learns," do you affirm that
this is the least and first speech?

---

[6]The word for "noun" here, *onoma*, also means "name." See 261D.

D *Theaetetus:* I do.

Stranger: For now, I suppose, he indicates something about the things that *are* or come to be or have come to be or will come to be. He doesn't merely name but brings something to closure by weaving together verbs with nouns. Hence we say that he speaks and does not merely name; what's more, we utter the name "speech" for this weaving.

Theaetetus: Correct.

Stranger: And so—just as with things, some fitted together and others didn't—so too with vocal signs, some don't fit together while others,
E by fitting together, produce speech.

Theaetetus: That's altogether so.

Stranger: Then there's this further little thing.

Theaetetus: What's that?

Stranger: Whenever there is speech, it's necessary that it be speech about something, and impossible for it not to be about anything.

Theaetetus: Just so.

Stranger: And mustn't it also be of a certain quality?

Theaetetus: Of course.

Stranger: Then let's pay close attention to one another.

Theaetetus: We must.

Stranger: Well then, I'll make you a speech by putting together thing and action through noun and verb. And you tell me what the speech is about.

263 A *Theaetetus:* I'll do what I can.

Stranger: "Theaetetus sits." Not a long speech, is it?

Theaetetus: No—it's quite measured.

Stranger: Now it's your job to say both what it's about and what its subject is.

Theaetetus: Plainly, it's about me and I'm the subject as well.

Stranger: And what about this one?

Theaetetus: Which one?

Stranger: "Theaetetus, with whom I am now conversing, flies."

Theaetetus: Here too no one would say anything other than that I'm the subject and that it's about me as well.

Stranger: But we say that it's necessary for each of our speeches to be of a certain quality.

B *Theaetetus:* Yes.

Stranger: Now of what quality should we say each of these two speeches is?

Theaetetus: The one is false, I suppose, while the other is true.

Stranger: The true one of them says about you things that *are*, as they *are*.

Theaetetus: Certainly.

Stranger: And the false one says things other than the things that *are*.

Theaetetus: Yes.

Stranger: Then it says things that *are not* as if they *were*.

Theaetetus: Just about.

Stranger: And it says about you things that *are*, which are other than the things that *are*. For we were claiming, I suppose, that with regard to each thing many things *are*, and many other things *are not*.

Theaetetus: Exactly.

C *Stranger:* Now as for the latter speech I gave about you, it is first of all and with the utmost necessarity one of the shortest from among those we marked off as speech—whatever it is.

Theaetetus: At least that's what we agreed on just now.

Stranger: And secondly, it indeed has a subject.

Theaetetus: Just so.

Stranger: And if you aren't the subject, then there's no other subject whatsoever.

Theaetetus: Of course.

Stranger: But if there's no subject, then there's no speech at all. For we declared that it was in the realm of impossibilities for a speech to be a speech that was of nothing at all.

Theaetetus: Most correct.

D *Stranger:* Now when things are said about you, and yet things that are other are said as the same and things that *are not* as things that *are*, it seems altogether the case that when this sort of composition arises out of both verbs and nouns, there arises a speech that is truly and in its very being *false*.

Theaetetus: Very true.

Stranger: But what then: Isn't it already manifest that these kinds—thinking and opinion and also appearance—all arise in our souls as false as well as true?

Theaetetus: How's that?

Stranger: You'll understand more easily if you first grasp whatever
E each *is* and how they differ from one another.

Theaetetus: Just give me the chance.

Stranger: Well then, aren't thinking and speech the same, except
that the soul's inner conversation with itself, when it arises without
voice, has been given just this title by us—"thinking"?

Theaetetus: By all means.

Stranger: But has the stream that issues forth from the soul and
goes through the mouth by means of sound been called "speech"?

Theaetetus: True.

Stranger: And what's more, we know that in our speeches there is—

Theaetetus: What?

Stranger: Both affirmation and negation.

Theaetetus: We do know that.

264 A *Stranger:* Then when this arises in the soul in accordance with thinking and in silence, can you call it anything but "opinion"?

Theaetetus: Of course not.

Stranger: And again, when such a condition is present to anyone not
by itself but through perception, can it correctly be called anything
other than "appearance"?

Theaetetus: No.

Stranger: Therefore, since speech was true *and* false, and in the realm
of speech thinking appeared as a conversation of the soul with itself,
B and opinion is the completion of thinking, and what we mean by "it
appears" is an intermixing of perception and opinion, it's necessary—
since these are akin to speech—that some of them are sometimes false.

Theaetetus: Of course.

Stranger: Do you notice then that false opinion and speech were found
sooner than we'd anticipated when we were afraid just now that by seeking them we'd be throwing ourselves into an altogether endless task?

Theaetetus: I do notice.

Stranger: Therefore let's not grow dispirited about the rest of the
C search. For since this has become clear, let's recollect our earlier
divisions according to forms.

Theaetetus: What divisions?

Stranger: We divided the image-making expertise into two forms, likeness-making and apparition-making.

Theaetetus: Yes.

Stranger: And we said that we were at an impasse about the sophist—into which of these we should put him.

Theaetetus: That's how it was.

Stranger: And as we were at this impasse, an even greater dizziness engulfed us, when an argument appeared that disputes with everyone:
D that likeness or image or apparition would be nothing at all because the false *is* nowise never nowhere.

Theaetetus: What you say is true.

Stranger: And now, since it's come to light that false speech *is*, and it's also come to light that false opinion *is*, there's room to *be* for imitations of the things that *are*, and room for a deceiving expertise to arise from this state of affairs.

Theaetetus: There's room.

Stranger: And we did in fact come to an agreement in our earlier discussions that the sophist was in one or the other of these divisions.

Theaetetus: Yes.

Stranger: Let us therefore try again to pass onward. Let's split the
E proposed kind in two, always keeping to the right hand part of the section and hold fast to the community to which the sophist belongs, until we've stripped away all his common features and left him his
265 A indwelling nature. Then we may show him forth, first to ourselves and next to those who are by nature nearest in kind to such a Way.

Theaetetus: Right.

Stranger: Some time ago we began with the division between the making and the getting expertise, didn't we?

Theaetetus: Yes.

Stranger: And the sophist made his appearance to us in forms of getting such as hunting and competing and trading?

Theaetetus: By all means.

Stranger: But since at this point the imitative art has embraced him, it's clear that we must first divide the making art itself into two. For
B I suppose that imitating is a sort of making, although of images, we say, and not of each of the things themselves. Right?

Theaetetus: That's altogether so.

Stranger: So let there first be two parts of making.

Theaetetus: What are they?

Stranger: One is divine, the other human.

Theaetetus: I haven't understood yet.

Stranger: We claimed—if indeed we remember what was said at the beginning—that every power that becomes a cause of the coming to be afterward of what was not there beforehand is a power of making.

Theaetetus: We remember.

C *Stranger:* Then all the animals that are mortal, and all the growths that grow on the earth from seeds and roots, and all the soulless bodies, fusible and not, that are put together within the earth—will we claim that these things, which were not there beforehand, come to be afterward from anything other than a god working as a craftsman? Or availing ourselves of the opinion and talk of most men—

Theaetetus: What opinion?

Stranger: The opinion that nature begets these things from some cause that is spontaneous and that grows them without thinking. Or will we claim that the cause arises with reason and divine knowledge from god?

D *Theaetetus:* I often go back and forth between the two opinions, perhaps because of my age. Yet now, as I look at you and gather that you think they come to be in accordance with god, I myself also adopt this belief.

Stranger: Beautifully said, Theaetetus. And if we believed you were one of those who would somehow opine otherwise at a later time, we'd now attempt to make you agree by using argument together with compelling persuasion. But since I understand your nature thoroughly—

E that even without our arguments it moves on its own toward the very things you now say pull you—I'll let it go. For it would take too much time. Instead, I'll suppose that things said to be by nature are made by divine art, while what's put together by men from these things is made by human art, and that according to this account the making art is of two kinds, one human and one divine.

Theaetetus: Right.

Stranger: Then since these are two, cut each of the two again in two.

Theaetetus: How?

266 A *Stranger:* Earlier you cut the whole of the making art widthwise, as it were, while now you must cut it again, this time lengthwise.

Theaetetus: Let it have been cut.

Stranger: In this way there come to be exactly four parts of it in all: two parts on our side are human, while two other parts on the gods' side are divine.

Theaetetus: Yes.

Stranger: But when in turn they are divided in the other way, one part from each of the two parts is "thing-itself-making," while the pair of parts left over would pretty much be called "image-making." And so in this way the making art is again divided in two.

B *Theaetetus:* Say once more how each of the two is divided.

Stranger: We know that we, I suppose, and the other animals, along with the elements from which these have sprouted—fire and water and their kin—all individually are the offspring and finished products of a god. Or how is it?

Theaetetus: Just so.

Stranger: And images of each of these individual things, which are not the things themselves, follow along, these too having arisen through superhuman contrivance.

Theaetetus: What are they?

Stranger: Apparitions, the ones said to be "self-sprung." I mean both those in our dreams and all those that occur in the daytime: a
C shadow whenever darkness arises in firelight, or when twofold light, the indwelling and the foreign—coalescing on bright and smooth surfaces and affording a perception contrary to our previously accustomed sight— produces a form.[7]

Theaetetus: Yes, these are two works of divine making: the thing itself and the image that accompanies each.

Stranger: And what about *our* art: Won't we declare that we make a house itself by means of the housebuilding art, whereas by means of painting we make another house, produced as a kind of man-made dream for those who are awake?

D *Theaetetus:* By all means.

Stranger: Then in the same way, all the other works of our "making-action" are in turn twofold and go in pairs: the one is a thing itself, made, we claim, by the "thing-itself-making" art, while the other is an image, made by the image-making art.

Theaetetus: Now I understand better; and I posit two forms of making, each of which is cut in two. According to one way of cutting, there's the divine and the human; while according to the other, the one cut is composed of things themselves, while the other, its offspring, is composed of certain semblances of them.

E *Stranger:* Let's recollect, moreover, that of image-working there

---

[7]See *Timaeus* 46B, *Theaetetus* 193 C-D and Cornford, p. 327.

was to be the likeness-making kind on the one hand and the apparition-making kind on the other, on the condition that the false come to light as genuinely false and as by nature some distinct *one* among the things that *are*.

Theaetetus: That was so.

Stranger: So then, didn't the genuinely false come to light among the things that *are*? And for this reason, won't we now indisputably count off the kinds of image-making as two?

Theaetetus: Yes.

267   A   *Stranger:* Let us therefore once again mark off apparition-making into two.

Theaetetus: How?

Stranger: One part comes to be through instruments, while the other comes about when the very maker of the apparition furnishes himself as instrument.

Theaetetus: What do you mean?

Stranger: I have in mind when someone uses his own body to make it appear to resemble your figure, or to make his voice like your voice—this part of the apparition-making art has especially been called, I suppose, "imitating."

Theaetetus: Yes.

Stranger: So by addressing this part of the art as "imitative," let's appropriate it. And let's go easy on ourselves by setting everything else
    B   aside and letting another collect it into one and give it a fitting title.

Theaetetus: So let the one be appropriated, the other set aside.

Stranger: And surely it's worth considering this part again as twofold, Theaetetus. Look why that is.

Theaetetus: Tell me.

Stranger: Some of those who imitate do it knowing what they are imitating, others not knowing. And yet, what greater division shall we posit than that between non-recognition and recognition?

Theaetetus: None at all.

Stranger: Wasn't the imitation we just spoke of on the part of those who know? For someone who imitated you would recognize your figure and you?

    C   *Theaetetus:* Of course.

Stranger: But what about the figure of justice and of virtue taken as a whole? Aren't there people who are ignorant of it but opine it in some way, and who try very ardently to make this seeming figure appear as if it were within them, by imitating it as best they can in deeds and words?

Theaetetus: There are very many such people.

Stranger: Do they all fail to seem to be just, even though they aren't at all? Or is it completely the contrary?

Theaetetus: Completely.

Stranger: Well then, I think we must say that this imitator who is D ignorant is other than the one who recognizes.

Theaetetus: Yes.

Stranger: Where then will one get hold of a fitting name for either of them? Or isn't it very clear that that's hard, because with respect to the division of kinds into forms, there was, it seems, a certain ancient and also scatterbrained laziness among our forerunners, so that no one even tried to make the division. Therefore we cannot be extremely well-provided with names. Just the same—even if our language is rather daring—for the sake of discriminating, let's call the imitating based on E opinion the "opino-imitative" art and the one based on knowledge some sort of "informed" imitating.

Theaetetus: Let it be that.

Stranger: Therefore we must use not the informed sort but the other. For the sophist wasn't among those who know but in fact among those who imitate.

Theaetetus: Very much so.

Stranger: Then let's look at the opino-imitator as if he were an iron ingot to see if he's sound or if he's still got some twofold seam within himself.

Theaetetus: Let's look.

268 A *Stranger:* Well then, he's got a very marked seam. For one of them is naive, because he thinks he knows the things that he opines. But the figure of the other—because of his mucking about among arguments—contains much suspicion and fear that he's ignorant of those things about which he's presented himself to others in the figure of a knower.

Theaetetus: There certainly are men of each kind you've mentioned.

Stranger: Then shall we posit the one as a sort of simple imitator, the other as a dissembling imitator?[8]

Theaetetus: That's likely.

Stranger: But shall we say that the kind to which the latter belongs

---

[8] "Dissembling" here is *eirōnikon,* the origin of our English "ironic." In other dialogues it is sometimes applied to Socrates.

is in turn one or two?

Theaetetus: See for yourself.

B   *Stranger:* I'm looking. And a pair of men show themselves to me. I see one who can dissemble in public and with long speeches to multitudes, another who can do it in private and with short speeches by compelling the man with whom he converses to contradict himself.

Theaetetus: Very correctly spoken.

Stranger: Then whom shall we declare the maker of longer speeches to be? Statesman or demagogue?

Theaetetus: Demagogue.

Stranger: And what shall we call the other man? Wise or sophistical?

Theaetetus: I suppose it's impossible to call him wise, since we set him

C   down as not knowing. But since he's an imitator of the wise man, it's clear that he'll get a name derived from him. And I've now pretty nearly understood that we must truly address this man as that very one who is in every way and in his very being the Sophist or Professor of Wisdom.

Stranger: Then shall we tie up his name, just as we did earlier, by weaving it together from end to beginning?

Theaetetus: By all means.

Stranger: The man, then, who has arisen from the contradiction-making art of the dissembling part of the opining art—the imitative man— who himself has sprung from the apparition-making kind descended

D   from the image-making art and has marked off for himself the portion of making, not divine but human, that makes wonders in speeches—whoever claims that the sophist in his very being is of this "breed and blood"[9] will, it seems, speak the very truth.

Theaetetus: That's altogether so.

---

[9] Homer, *Iliad* VI. 211: a young warrior, after boasting of his lineage, foolishly exchanges gold for bronze.

GLOSSARY

This glossary is not arranged as an alphabetical list of Greek terms with English equivalents and definitions, but presents words in the way we thought about them—in clusters of associated meanings. Our hope is that readers will use the glossary not only to find out our translation of Greek words—many of which are recognizable in transliteration—but also as an introduction to the basic vocabulary of philosophical inquiry.

* * * * *

learning (*máthēsis*), the **learnable** (*máthēma*)

Mathesis is the activity of learning. It comes from the verb *manthánein*, which means both to learn and to understand, and is the origin of the word "mathematics." A *mathema* is anything learned, as in a lesson, study or intellectual discipline such as geometry or astronomy. We have translated it throughout as a "learnable," for example, a "soul-related learnable."

knowledge (*epistḗmē*), **know** (*epístasthai, eidénai*), **recognition** (*gnôsis*), **recognize** (*gignôskein*)

Episteme is the Greek word for knowledge in the sense of an accomplished, articulable understanding of a specific subject matter. Like *mathema* it refers to a discipline such as geometry and astronomy. It bears some similarity to what we call "science." We have translated *episteme* as "knowledge." The noun *episteme* comes from the verb *epistasthai*, which means to be knowledgable or expert. Its root meaning—from *epí* ("on" or "upon") and *hístasthai* ("to stand")—refers to someone who is, as we say, "on top of the material."

Gnosis is knowledge in the sense of acquaintance or recognition. It comes from the verb *gignoskein*, which can mean "come to know," "perceive," "discern," "observe" or "judge to be the case." To distinguish *gnosis* from *episteme*, we have translated it as "recognition." The verb *gignoskein* has been translated throughout as "recognize."

Eidenai means "know" in the sense of "know that something is the case" or "know how to do something." In its absolute sense, *eidenai* means generally to be knowledgeable or "savvy." The most interesting feature of *eidenai* is that it is the perfect form of the verb *horan*, "to see." Just as an *eidos* (see below) is something seen, "to know" is "to have seen."

wisdom (*sophía*), **thoughtfulness** (*phrónēsis*)

The original meaning of *sophia* or wisdom was excellence in the art of making something, for example, in the art of sculpture. In its later meaning

85

sophia is something like intellectual completeness regarding the highest, deepest and most comprehensive objects of inquiry. If wisdom in this sense can be called knowledge, then it is knowledge not of this or that but of the Whole. *Phronesis* is mindfulness, above all in the sense of practical or moral intelligence. We have translated it "thoughtfulness" to distinguish it from *sophia*. Similarly, *sophós* appears as "wise" and *phrónimos* as "thoughtful."

sophist *(sophistés)*, philosopher *(philósophos)*

"Sophist" and "philosopher" derive from two different relations to wisdom, *sophia* . The sophist is a professor of wisdom, that is, one who publicly claims to be wise; the philosopher by contrast is a lover of wisdom (from *phileín*, "to love"), one who claims not to possess but to desire wisdom. In a few places we have used the translations "professor of wisdom" and "lover of wisdom" to bring out the root meaning of the names.

stranger *(xénos)*

Xenos means both guest and host, that is, any of two parties bound by ties of hospitality. More particularly, a *xenos* is someone from a foreign city or land, with whom one is on friendly terms and to whom one owes cordial and respectful treatment. *Xenos* in this sense can be translated as either "guest" or "stranger." The traditional rendering "stranger" captures the stranger's foreignness and also suggests the welcoming tone of the Old West greeting: "Howdy, stranger, what brings you to town?" The importance of treating guests properly is indicated by Homer's epithet, *Zeus xénios*, "Zeus, the patron god of strangers."

education *(paideía)*; joke *(paidía)*

The word we consistently translate as "joke," *paidia*, comes from the word for child (or slave), *pais*. *Paidia* is often contrasted with *spoudé*, seriousness, and hence in certain contexts might have been translated as playfulness or even child's play. *Paidia* sounds like another word that comes from *pais*, the word for the serious activity in which both the sophist and the stranger from Elea are engaged: *paideia* (education). Needless to say, Plato takes full advantage of the kinship between *paidia* and *paideia*.

* * * * *

art or expertise *(téchnē)*, expert *(technítēs)*, layman *(idiótēs)*, terrible or terrific *(deinós)*

Techne is any teachable, specialized and publicly acknowledged know-how. Characterized by its method and cunning (compare the English "technique"), *techne* can refer to anything from mathematics to the bath attendant's art. A *technites* is an expert in or practitioner of this know-how. The non-expert is *átechnos*—a man without an art. Sometimes the stranger refers to him as an *idiotes* (the origin of our English "idiot"), a private man who lacks professional skill. We have rendered techne as either "art" or "expertise."

The adjective *deinos* (from *déos,* "fear") can mean terrible, powerful, wondrous, strange or clever. Like the word "terrific" in English, *deinos* can be used as a term of admiration, for example when we say that someone is "terrific" or "terribly good" at something, especially an art. We have translated it according to context as either "terrible," "terrific" or "awesome."

doing or **making** (*poíēsis*), **do** or **make** (*poiein*), **be affected, suffer** or **experience** (*páschein*), **action** or **business** (*práxis*)

Poiesis, from which we get our English "poetry," is from the verb *poiein,* "do" or "make." *Paschein,* the correlative of *poiein,* means "receive an impression from without" and so "suffer" or "undergo." Whereas *poiein* is a doing, *paschein* is a being done to. We have translated it as "be affected." *Praxis* refers to any doing, transaction or business (compare the English "practice" and "practical"). It derives from the verb *práttein,* which means "achieve" or "accomplish."

power (*dýnamis*), **job** or **deed** (*érgon*), **produce** (*apergázesthai*)

Dynamis is any power, strength or capacity (compare the English "dynamic" and "dynamite"). We have translated it as "power." The verbal form *dýnasthai* means "to be able." A man without an art may nevertheless have some sort of *dynamis.* Furthermore, the ability to be affected and moved is no less a *dynamis* than the ability to affect and move.

Ergon has a variety of meanings in the *Sophist* . Its basic meaning is that of work—work as activity rather than mere labor. When *ergon* seems to refer to the sophist's professionalism, we have translated it as "job," that is, as a publicly recognized occupation. When contrasted with *logos,* "speech," *ergon* appears as "deed." The verb *apergázesthai,* which occurs often in the dialogue, refers to the act of "finishing off," that is, working something up to a condition of fullness or completion. It has been rendered as "produce."

* * * * *

way (*méthodos*), **passage** (*póros*), **impasse** or **perplexity** (*aporía*)

Throughout the *Sophist* inquisitive speech is playfully compared to bodily motion in space and time. To bring out this imitation of a journey, we have tried to be faithful to words whose root meaning suggests place or passage. The word *methodos,* from which we get our English "method," has been translated "way" to bring out the meaning of *hodós* as way or path: a method is literally the way after (*metá*) something, that is, a pursuit. We have sometimes used the capitalized Way to bring out the solemn and somewhat comic formality with which the stranger speaks of his and Theaetetus' *methodos*.

Closely related to *hodos* and *methodos* is *poros*. In its literal meaning, a *poros* is a ford, a means of crossing a river. It can also mean a channel or passageway for ships. The verb *poreúesthai* means "to make one's way" or "to proceed." Most generally, a *poros* is any sort of means, device or contrivance. Something is *eúporos* when it allows for easy passage, while *aporia* is an impasse, a condition of blockage. In the sphere of inquiry, *aporia* is perplexity, the lack of some means of overcoming a problem or dilemma. We have used both "impasse" and "perplexity" as translations of aporia.

declare or **claim** (*phánai*), **say** or **speak** (*légein*), **converse** (*dialégesthai*), **debate** (*antilégein*), **account, argument, speech** or **reason** (*lógos*)

As befits a dialogue in which the relation between being and speaking is so central an issue, the *Sophist* is filled with verbs that refer to one manner or another of speaking: *onomázein* (name), *eponomázein* (title), *prosagoreúein* (address), *kaleín* (call) and so on. Among these many verbs, two deserve notice: *legein*, the root meaning of which is "gather" or "select," and *phanai*, a relative of both *phaínein* (bring to light, appear) and *phýsis* (nature). The first we generally translate as "say" or "speak," the second as "declare" or "claim." Two verbs derived from *legein* are frequently used in the dialogue: *dialegesthai* (literally, "to talk through") and *antilegein* (literally, "to talk against" as in an argument).

Logos is the noun that corresponds to *legein* . It has a number of meanings: sentence, speech, argument, thought and even ratio. At the root of each of these meanings lie the notions of gathering and selecting, of separating and weaving together. We translate it "account," "argument," "speech" and in one case (235C), "reason."

divide (*diairéin*), **separate** or **discern** (*diakrínein*)

The verb *diairein* literally means "to take apart" (*dia + hairein*). It can refer to cutting some object, e.g., a line, or to distinguishing in thought or speech the parts of some subject-matter. We always translate it and words related to it with some form of the word "divide." The verb *diakrinein* (related to the English discern) has roughly the same range of meaning as *diairein*, though it perhaps emphasizes somewhat more the notion of distinguishing in thought. We translate it and words related to it with some form of the words "separate" and "discern."

boundary (*hóros*), **mark off** (*diorízein*)

A *horos* is a limit or border; the related verb *diorizein* (from *diá* + *horízein*) means to separate or mark off a territory by means of a boundary, as a horizon bounds our view. These words come to mean respectively "definition" and "to define." In this dialogue, however, the participants are not yet limited to defining concepts or words; instead they are staking out divisions within the field of beings and activities.

* * * * *

form (*eídos*), **look** (*idéa*), **kind** (*génos*)

The word we translate as "form," *eidos*, is a central term in the dialogues. Its root, [w]id (as in our "video"), refers to vision. *Eidos* is the form or shape or aspect that presents itself to either physical or intellectual sight; it is that by which things can be recognized. Derived from the perfect of the verb "to see," *eidos* suggests perfected or complete visibility. The related word *idea* means, similarly, the characteristic look of a thing, that by which it can be known as just the thing it is. It does not mean "idea" in our sense, something that exists only in the mind.

Genos is derived from *gígnesthai*, the verb for coming to be and being born. A *genos* may a group of members akin through common birth or generation, or it may be the common character shared by those members. Therefore we translate it as "kind" (a word related to kin and kindred) and once, in the very first speech, as "kin."

The Latin translations of *genos* and *eidos* are "genus" and "species;" these become technical terms used in the method of classification for which the *Sophist* lays the philosophical foundation.

beginning (*archḗ*)

An *arche* is an origin or beginning, either in the sense of a temporal starting-point or in the sense of a source or governing principle. It can also mean governing power or sovereignty. Its corresponding verb *archein* can mean either to make a beginning or to rule. We have translated *arche* as "beginning." The reader must keep in mind that this word, even when it means "beginning" in the temporal sense, has strong overtones of "source" and "ruling principle."

becoming (*génesis*)

Genesis is derived from the verb *gígnesthai*, a verb that can mean "come to be" or "be born" (see *genos* above), or more generally "happen" in the sense of "arise" or "come about." Like *arche*, *genesis* can mean origin or source. It can also refer to someone's birth, race or descent. Unlike *arche*, *genesis* suggests not only origin but origination (as in the English "genesis"), that is, the ongoing act and process of coming to be. We have translated it as "becoming."

nature (*phýsis*)

Physis or "nature" covers a wide range of meanings in Greek. It encompasses the natural qualities, powers or condition of something or someone. It can refer to a human being's "bent" or natural disposition, for example when we say: "That's his nature." It can also refer to someone's outward appearance or stature. Another meaning is nature in the sense of kind, sort or species: lion, ox, male, female would be examples of different "natures." More generally, *physis* can mean the indwelling order or constitution of something, the internal principle by which all natural things things things grow and move, or even the whole of all generated things.

Physis comes from the verb *phýein*, which means "bring forth" or "come forth" in the sense of "sprout." The Latin *natura*, the origin of our "nature," derives from the verb *nascor*, which means "to be born" and thus captures *phyein* in the sense of "come forth" or "arise." Related to the verb *phainein* (see below), *phýein* can also mean "show forth" or "bring to light." The passive form *phýesthai* means "to spring up or arise." We have translated it as "crop up." The perfect form *péphyke* means something like "is that way by nature."

Being (*to on*), beinghood (*ousía*), Non-being (*to mē on*), the things that *are* or beings (*ta ónta*), being (*on*), non-being (*mē on*), not-being (*ouk on*); genuinely or in its [very] being (*óntōs*)

There are two expressions in the dialogue for which Being would be an appropriate translation: *ousia* and *to on*. We decided to let it be our rendering of *to on*. *To on* is the neuter participial form of "to be" coupled with the kind-signalling definite article, and it rather than *ousia* regularly turns up in conjunction with other "greatest kinds" in the dialogue. *Ousia* by contrast is a noun derived from the feminine form of the participle and in this dialogue tends to be conjoined with *genesis*, becoming.

In ordinary Greek *ousia* means "property" or "real estate," above all the homestead without which a human being is nothing. We translate it by the somewhat peculiar sounding "beinghood," since "-hood," better than the abstract "-ness," seemed to capture the sense of fullness, of intensification, implicit in *ousia*: consider "manhood" or "neighborhood."

There are two negative particles in Greek, *mē* and *ou* (or *ouk*). As a rule, when *mē* negates a participle, it signals a less definite, less determinate, form of negation than *ou*. "Not-" for *ou* and "non-" for *mē* are our attempt to bring this distinction over into English.

Unfortunately, *ontos* (literally "beingly"), the adverb derived from the participle *on*, cannot be directly translated into English. We have adopted three renderings: "in its being," "in its very being" and on certain occasions "genuinely."

motion (*kínēsis*), **rest** (*stásis*)

Kinesis means not only motion in space and time but also other kinds of change such as growth. We chose "motion" as a term in normal use and somewhat broader than "locomotion." *Stasis* as the contrary of motion is translated as "rest," meant not in the sense of a lack of or a cessation of motion, but as an original, independent condition. *Stasis* comes from the Greek verb "to stand," and "stand-still" or "stationariness" would have been an accurate, though strained, rendition. *Stasis* also means a stand or position, hence a party or faction, and thence factional strife; it is sometimes translated "sedition."

the Same (*tautón*), **the Other** (*tháteron*)

The word we translate as "the Same" comes from the word *autós*, as in automobile and autonomy. When used adjectivally, *autos* serves to intensify or emphasize the word it modifies: *autós Sōcrátēs* means "Socrates himself." When preceded by the definite article, *autos* is the ordinary Greek expression for the same: to say that Socrates is the same man he always was is to say that the man himself, the very man, hasn't changed. Treated as a kind, *tauton* (= *to* + *auto*) is thus the principle of selfhood; it is that through which or by which each thing is just the thing it is.

The word we translate as "the Other" (*thateron*) comes from the word *héteros* (*thateron* = *to* + *heteron*). In contrast to *állos*, which signifies what is different from any number of things, what is indifferently other, *heteros* always means what is other than an other, the other *of two* (as in "heterosexual"), although one of the terms may be indefinitely other (as in "heterodox"). Treated as a kind, *thateron* is thus the principle of negative pairing; it is that through which or by which each thing is at once in relation to and separated off from some one other thing.

It is worth mentioning, in this context, that Greek nouns, adjectives and verbs admit of a *dual* as well as singular and plural forms. Such forms are relatively rare in the Greek of Plato's time and are ordinarily used of natural pairs: hands, eyes and so on. Yet in the *Sophist* dual forms turn up everywhere. We have tried in each case to mark their presence by such expressions as "a pair of" or "the two of."

participate (*metéchein*), **participation** (*méthexis*); **commune** (*koinōneín*), **community** (*koinōnía*)

There are four verbs in the dialogue that refer to the activity of partaking or communing, so central to the stranger's account of the "greatest kinds:" *metechein*, *metalambánein*, *meteínai* and *koinonein*. We have translated them, respectively, as "participate," "have a share in," "partake" and "commune." The two that occur most often are *metechein* and *koinonein*. Their corresponding nouns—*methexis* and *koinonia*—have been rendered, respectively, "participation" and "community."

* * * * *

seem (*dokeín*), **opinion** (*dóxa*), **opine** (*doxázein*)

The verb *dokein* means "seem," "seem good or right," "appear" (as opposed to "be"), also "to have the opinion that. . . ." *Doxa*, derived from it, means both one's own opinion and the opinion others have of one, one's reputation. In the Platonic dialogues it often means an unfounded or mere opinion or seeming. The verb derived from *doxa*, *doxazein*, we translate "opine" to avoid the religious connotation of "believe." The ordinary usage closest to *doxazein* is "have the opinion, believe, guess or feel that. . . ."

image (*eídōlon*), **likeness** (*eikōn*), **imitation** (*mímēma*), **imitative art** (*mímēsis*), **semblance** (*homoíōma*)

An *eidolon* (from which comes our word "idol") is a diminutive *eidos*, literally a little or diminished form, which is thus the "image" of its fuller original. An *eikon* (from which comes our word "icon") means a thing that is similar or like something, hence a pictorial "likeness." A *mimema* is a copy or an "imitation." It is the product of *mimesis* (a word used in English). Early on in the dialogue *mimesis* refers to the general art of imitation, but in later passages is restricted to mimicry or miming by means of the body or voice. A *homoioma* (from the adjective *hómoios*, "like") is something that is similar to or resembles something else, hence a "semblance."

appearance (*phantasía*), **apparition** (*phántasma*)

Phantasia is derived from a verb that is frequently used in the dialogue and is built on the word for light (*pháos* or *phōs*, as in our "photograph"). The verb *phaínein*, related to *phanai* (see above), can mean in its various forms: "bring to light," "come to light," "be manifest," hence "appear." A *phantasia* is therefore an appearance in a double sense; it is what comes to light and also what is manifest to us. In other contexts it can mean the capacity for inner appearances: "imagination," "phantasy." A *phantasma*, like our "phantasm," is an appearance that is sometimes artificial and often strange or distorted; hence our translation, "apparition."

BIBLIOGRAPHY

Texts and Translations Most Frequently Consulted:

Benardete, S. 1984. *Plato's Sophist*, Part II of The Being of the Beautiful: Translated and with Commentary. Chicago: The University of Chicago Press. (Has bibliography.)

Burnet, J. 1900. *Sophista* in *Platonis Opera*: Vol. I. Oxford: The Clarendon Press. (With critical apparatus.)

Campbell, L. 1867. *The* Sophistes *and Politicus of Plato, With a Revised Text and English Notes* . Oxford: Clarendon Press.

Cobb, W S. 1990. *Plato's* Sophist. Savage, MD: Rowman and Littlefield Publishers. (With analysis, notes and bibliography.)

Cornford, F. M. 1934, reprinted 1957. *Plato's Theory of Knowledge* : The Theaetetus *and the* Sophist: *Translated with a Running Commentary* . New York: The Liberal Arts Press.

Fowler, H. N. 1952, revised. *Plato*: Theaetetus *and* Sophist. Cambridge, MA: Loeb Library, Harvard University Press. (Facing Greek and English.)

Jowett, B. 1892. *Sophist* in *The Dialogues of Plato, Translated into English*, Vol. II. New York: Random House (1937). (With marginal notes.)

Robin, L. 1950. *Le Sophiste* in *Platon, Oeuvres Complètes, Traduction Nouvelle et Notes* . Paris: Bibliothèque de la Pléiade, Gallimard.

Schleiermacher, F. 1804-1810. *Sophistes* in *Platon* : *Sämtliche Werke*, Vol. 4, Edited by O. Walter, E. Grassi and G. Plamböck. Hamburg: Rowohlt (1958).

White, N. P. 1993. *Plato* : Sophist, *Translated with Introduction and Notes* . Indianapolis: Hackett Publishing Company. (Has bibliography.)

Selected Books on the *Sophist*:

Heidegger, M. 1924-25. *Platon*: Sophistes, *Gesamtausgabe*, Vol. 19, edited by Ingeborg Schüssler. Frankfurt: Vittorio Klostermann (1992).

Klein, J. 1977. *Plato's Trilogy*: Theaetetus, *the* Sophist *and the* Statesman. Chicago: The University of Chicago Press.

Rosen, S. 1983. *Plato's* Sophist: *The Drama of Original and Image*. New Haven: Yale University Press. (Has bibliography.)